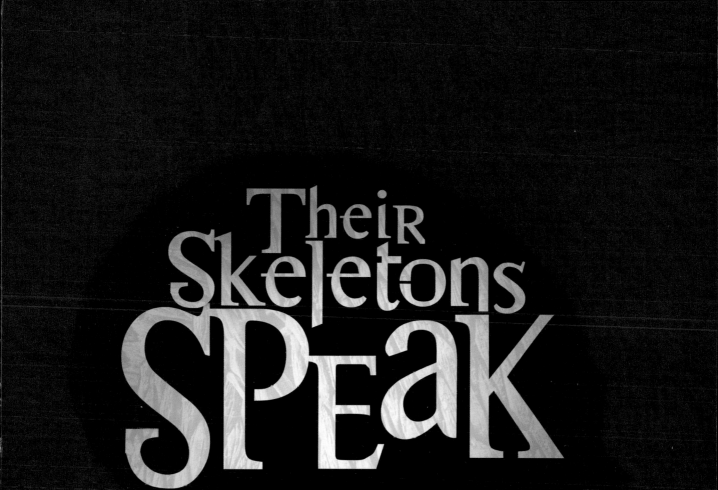

Their Skeletons Speak

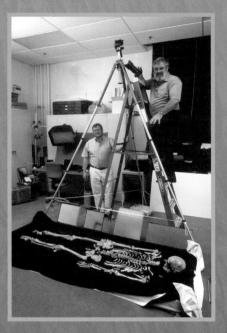

In memory of Chip Clark—
gifted artist, treasured friend.

His photographs sow wonder.

—S.M.W. and D.W.O.

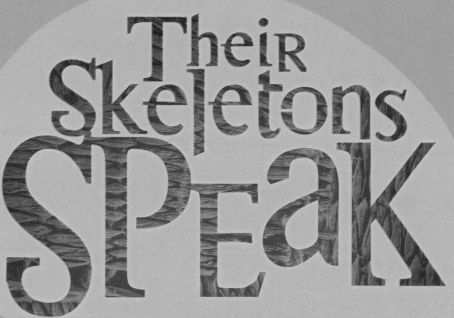

Their Skeletons Speak

KENNEWICK MAN AND THE PALEOAMERICAN WORLD

SALLY M.
WALKER

DOUGLAS W.
OWSLEY

🍃 CAROLRHODA BOOKS | MINNEAPOLIS

Carolrhoda Books
A division of Lerner Publishing Group, Inc.
241 First Avenue North
Minneapolis, MN 55401 U.S.A.

Website address: www.lernerbooks.com

Main body text set in Rotis Serif Std 11.5/15.
Typeface provided by Adobe Systems.

Library of Congress Cataloging-in-Publication Data

Walker, Sally M.
    Their skeletons speak : Kennewick man and the Paleoamerican world / by
Sally M. Walker and Douglas W. Owsley.
        p.   cm.
    Includes bibliographical references and index.
    ISBN 978-0-7613-7457-2 (lib. bdg. : alk. paper)
    1. Kennewick Man. 2. Human remains (Archaeology)—Washington
(State) 3. Paleo-Indians—Washington (State)—Origin. 4. Paleo-Indians—
Anthropometry—Washington (State) 5. Indians of North America—Washington
(State)—Antiquities. 6. Washington (State)—Antiquities. I. Owsley, Douglas W.
II. Title.
    E78.W3W23 2012
    970.01'1—dc23   2011051329

Manufactured in the United States of America
1 – PP – 7/15/12

Contents

Where to BEGin

THIS STORY ABOUT BONES BEGINS WITH A DAM. McNary Dam spans the Columbia River about 45 miles (72 km) downstream from Kennewick, Washington. Because a dam, by definition, constrains the flow of water, it can't be placed at the beginning of a river. It must be located elsewhere along a river's course—perhaps someplace in the middle. And oddly, for the bones in this tale, picking up the story somewhere in the middle makes sense.

Among other things, McNary Dam regulates the water flow of the Columbia River. When the dam is closed, water pools behind it and creates Lake Wallula. Control of the dam—and thus the level of the river and the lake—rests with the Army Corps of Engineers, a federal agency that provides engineering services to the United States. At the end of July in 1996, the Corps of Engineers closed the dam for a very specific reason: so the delicate hulls of racing boats wouldn't hang up in the shallows as the craft sped through the water at over 200 miles (325 km) an hour.

Boats racing at that speed are sure to draw a crowd, and they did on that day in 1996. Thousands of people flocked to the banks of the Columbia, but only two of them would make the discovery of a lifetime and, by doing so, take all of us on a journey nine thousand years into the past.

That a boat race plays a role in this story may seem unlikely. But one of the things you learn when studying prehistoric human remains is that the story—especially one like this that flows through laboratories, archaeological sites, religious ceremonies, courtrooms, and police evidence lockers—seldom follows an obvious path. The biography of a famous historical figure might begin with birth, proceed through life, and conclude with death. However, neat beginnings, middles, and ends are luxuries seldom available to those who study prehistoric men and women. Instead, scientists examine and reexamine tantalizing but scattered clues about the people who lived long before written history. No possibility can go unconsidered because even the tiniest clue could be the thread that leads to an earthshaking discovery.

Even though this narrative begins with the discovery of bones, it is ultimately the tale of a human life, of a strong man who overcame great physical pain, of someone who was, above all, a survivor. It might also be part of a tale of how humans came to North America.

McNary Dam, on the Columbia River, is downstream from Kennewick, Washington.

CHAPTERONE

A Day at the Races

TWENTY-YEAR-OLD WILL THOMAS AND
NINETEEN-YEAR-OLD DAVE DEACY WERE TWO
OF THE THOUSANDS LURED BY RACING BOATS
TO COLUMBIA PARK ON SUNDAY, JULY 28, 1996.
They and a group of friends were on their way to
the Tri-City Water Follies, an event that brings elite
hydroplane boat racers to Kennewick, Washington.
Crowds lined the banks of the river, jockeying for
good places to view the Columbia Cup race.

"We were a bit late arriving, so we quickly
parked the truck and headed toward the main
entrance," recalled Will Thomas. Noticing the long
lines, Thomas and Deacy split from their friends
and walked along the river, seeking a spot where
they could watch the boats without having to wait
in line. After making their way across the grass
and through shrubs, they scrambled down the
riverbank's crumbly, 6-foot-high (2-meter) cliff,
splashed into the shallow water, and waded upriver.
That's when their real adventure began—one they

could never have imagined in a thousand years but one that had been waiting for at least nine thousand.

"I was wearing my flip-flops and walking in the water about twenty feet [6 m] offshore. I looked down through the water and saw a rock. All I could see was the top of the rock, which was round and enough like a human skull that I decided to use it to play a trick on Dave," said Thomas. "I reached down to pick up the rock, but it was stuck in the mud. It took me a minute to pull it loose. As soon as I picked it up, the first thing I saw was human teeth." Speechless, Thomas held the skull up to show Deacy, whose wide-opened eyes and dropped jaw mirrored Thomas's surprise.

They looked further around the area and saw more objects they thought might be bones. Deacy even picked one of them up—a piece that was long and brown, like a stick. They decided it probably was a stick, so they put it back in the water. Still shocked by their discovery, the two friends discussed what they'd found. From time to time, human bodies turn up in the Columbia River. Were these bones, perhaps, the remains of someone who had drowned? Or could something more sinister have occurred?

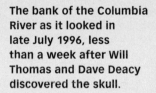

The bank of the Columbia River as it looked in late July 1996, less than a week after Will Thomas and Dave Deacy discovered the skull.

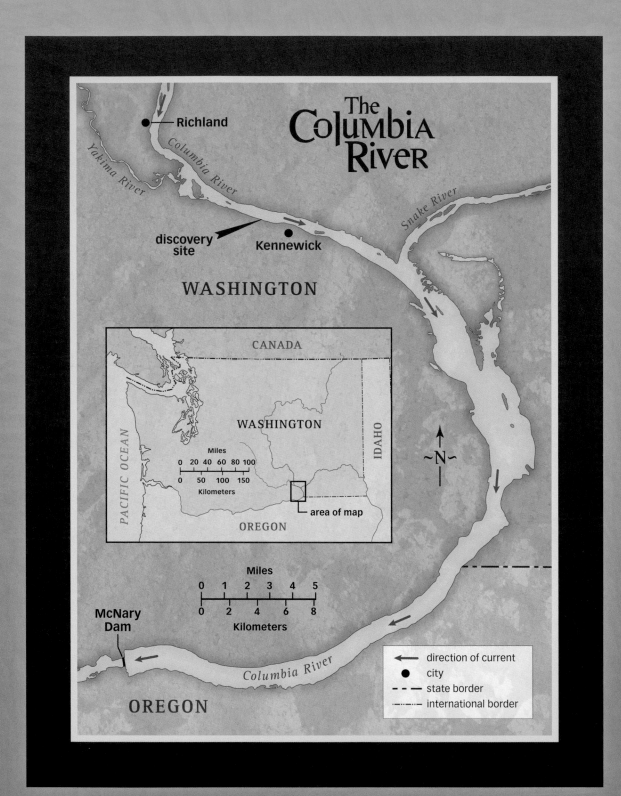

The Columbia River

Russian olive trees grow along the riverbank in that area of Columbia Park. The trees' long, daggerlike thorns discourage most people from pushing their way through the brush. But there were some signs of recent activity—broken bushes and a sketchy path. Were the remains those of a murder victim whose body had been dragged through the brush and then left in the river, where people were unlikely to stumble across it?

Thomas and Deacy knew they should tell the police, but they hadn't seen any in the area. They'd waited a whole year to watch the race. Leaving the river to search for an officer would mean missing the action. They discussed putting the skull back in the water and just leaving it but knew that would be wrong. The skull's condition clearly indicated the death hadn't occurred within the last few days. Maybe it would be okay to hold off telling the police for a few hours. Thomas and Deacy finally decided to leave the skull and retrieve it after the race, at which time they would search for a police officer. (In 1996 neither they nor their friends had cell phones, so a quick call wasn't possible.) The young men hid the skull on the riverbank, covering it with the long grasses that overhung the short, steep slope.

After the race was over, Thomas and Deacy collected the skull and put it in a bucket in the back of their friend's pickup truck. Heading toward home, they kept their eyes peeled for the police. Finally, they saw a squad car from the city of Richland. Thomas showed the police officer the skull and told him there were more bones in the river. Since the bones were near the border of the cities of Richland and Kennewick, the officer radioed for assistance from the Kennewick Police Department and the Benton County Sheriff's Office. This was only the first of many times the question arose about who would be responsible for these particular bones.

Returning to the river, the two young men and the officer awaited the other law enforcement personnel. Because the origin of the bones and the circumstances that led to their placement in the river were unknown, officials had to treat the remains and the area surrounding them as a possible crime scene.

At that point, the police also called Floyd Johnson, a former homicide detective. Since his retirement, he was serving as the Benton County coroner, a public officer who makes inquiries into deaths that may not have occurred by natural causes. If more bones were recovered, Johnson might be able to determine the cause of death.

SEARCH AND RECOVER

The search team motored upriver in a search-and-rescue boat. It had scarcely left shore before Deacy pointed out the spot where they'd hidden the skull.

Beaching the boat slightly beyond that area, the recovery team, including Floyd Johnson, searched the shallow water. They started picking up bones right away. One of them found the stick that Dave had discovered earlier. Everyone crowded around. Right away, Johnson knew it was a leg bone. "Dave and I were both surprised. It was a dark brown color and kind of coated with something sort of crusty. It still looked like a stick to us," Thomas said.

From the discussion among Johnson and the other members of the rescue team, Thomas realized the remains were not those of a person who had been alive recently. The general agreement was that the bones appeared old, but no one knew how old. With the bones and the possible crime scene secured, Thomas and Deacy were allowed to leave. Even as the young men were on their way home, Floyd Johnson considered a couple of things about the bones that baffled him. Thomas and Deacy had found the cranium— the upper part of the skull that

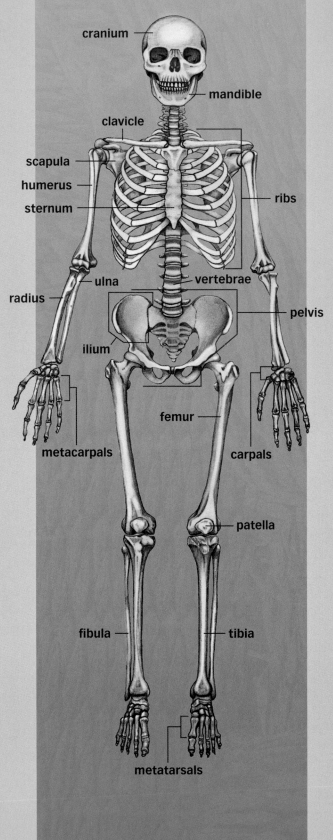

surrounds the brain. (The mandible, or lower jaw, was missing.) A femur, or thigh bone, was among the other bones the searchers had found. In the course of his work, Johnson had examined many craniums and femurs. However, these bones felt unusually heavy to Johnson—as if the passage of time had allowed sediment, or small grains of mud and sand, to infiltrate the bone. This, combined with the dark yellow-brown color of the bone, led him to think the remains might be at least a hundred years old.

One of the possibilities he considered was that the bones might be the remains of an Indian. More than once Indian remains had eroded from the banks of the Columbia River, washed out by lapping waves. They could also be the remains of a pioneer settler or farmer. Either way, it seemed the bones might tell an interesting tale.

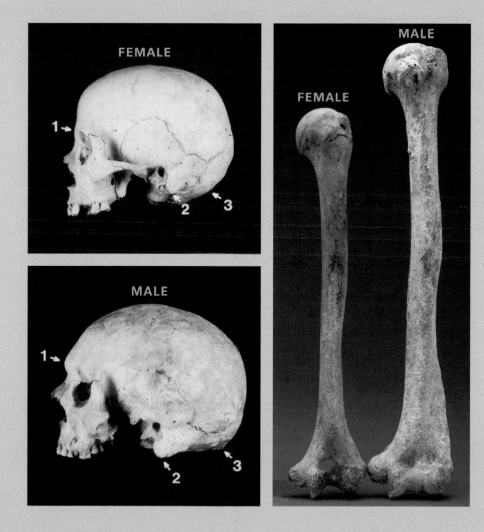

A few critical bones can allow a scientist to determine the gender of a set of remains. Humeri (upper arm bones, *right*) differ in length and thickness between men and women. Craniums (skulls, *left*) also differ between the sexes, with details of the male skull (marked 1, 2, and 3) more prominent than that of the female skull.

EXPERT OPINIONS

Seeking a definite answer, Johnson telephoned James Chatters, a local paleontologist and archaeologist. Johnson hoped Chatters's years of experience with bones—those of Native Americans and of white settlers—might quickly solve the puzzling story of these bones.

Receiving Johnson's call didn't surprise Chatters. "I was accustomed to calls like that. At that time I was serving as a forensic anthropologist [someone who studies bones] for the county, so they called me whenever bones turned up. Usually the bones are from a dog or a deer—those are common. Occasionally, though, the bones are human," Chatters recalled. He suggested Johnson bring the bones to his house, where he has a laboratory for examining them.

Standing in Chatters's yard, the two men looked into the white plastic bucket containing the bones. As he examined the skull and the teeth in the maxillae, or the two bones that form the upper jaw, Chatters agreed that the remains were indeed old. The teeth were worn to an extent

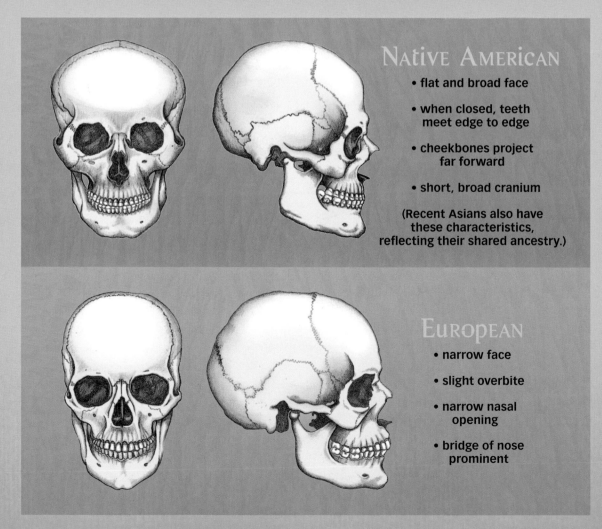

NATIVE AMERICAN

- flat and broad face

- when closed, teeth meet edge to edge

- cheekbones project far forward

- short, broad cranium

(Recent Asians also have these characteristics, reflecting their shared ancestry.)

EUROPEAN

- narrow face
- slight overbite
- narrow nasal opening
- bridge of nose prominent

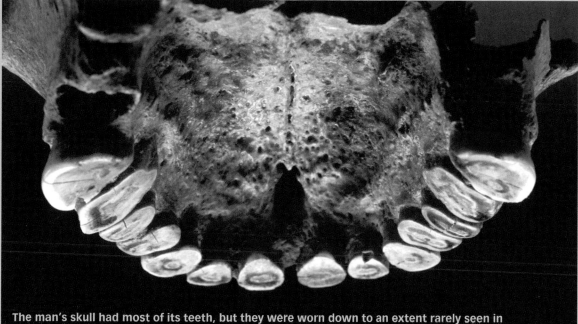

The man's skull had most of its teeth, but they were worn down to an extent rarely seen in contemporary skulls or in skulls from the recent past. These teeth are in the maxillae, or upper jaw.

seldom seen in modern people. They also agreed the remains were likely male. The size and shape of certain features of the skull—the prominent browridge and sloping forehead, for example—were characteristic of a man. Looking more closely, Chatters noted that the cranium's shape did not resemble any of the many Native American skulls he had seen. Like Johnson, he considered the possibility the remains were those of a pioneer settler. But the teeth didn't look like any settler's teeth Chatters had seen, and the skull didn't look truly European, as most settlers' would have.

For people with a trained eye, certain skull features—the cheekbones, for example—can provide clues about a skeleton's ancestry. This information can be critically important in helping us understand how and where past peoples lived. But each person is an individual and bone features within a particular population include many variations. Chatters knew not to rush to conclusions about the skull's ancestry based on a cursory inspection.

At Johnson's request, they returned to the scene so Chatters could examine the area. Perhaps Chatters would see a burial pit in the ground. Maybe he could find more bones. If they were really lucky, he might find bones protruding from the bank.

Back at the river, police officials continued their investigation. Chatters climbed into a boat and set off to the discovery site.

MORE BONES

By the time Chatters reached the site, it was after eight in the evening and the sunlight had grown dim. Chatters wondered if he would be able to see anything at all. "The first thing I did was to look at the riverbank and see if any more bones were in it," he said. He hoped to determine if the bones were still in situ—Latin for "in position," meaning an object is still lying in place where it originally laid. Bones that are in situ can offer information about how a person was buried. Artifacts, or man-made objects, found in situ help scientists visualize and understand ancient cultures and situations. Artifacts found in or near a grave may lead to the identification of the deceased individual's culture. Chatters didn't see more bones in the bank, so he shined his flashlight into the water.

At first, he saw only the bottom of the river. Then, a short distance away, something caught his eye when another searcher's light flickered across it. Two large pieces of bone gleamed against the dark mud. "The shadows were really quite stark. I was looking in the water and could see the two halves of the pelvis—the part of the skeleton formed by the bones of the hip and lower back—quite distinctly," said Chatters. Soft, sloppy, sandy mud slid from the pelvic bones as he lifted them from the water. But Chatters made no attempt to remove some hardened globs of sediment still adhering to the bones. He wanted to take a closer look at them in his laboratory. Perhaps similar sediment was nearby. With luck, he could compare sediment on the bones with sediment in the riverbank—and if they matched, maybe he could determine where the skeleton had originally been.

The pelvic bones quickly gave Chatters two pieces of information about the enigmatic remains. First, their large size told Chatters the individual had been an adult. Second, the shape indicated the individual was a man (female pelvises are shaped differently to allow for the birth of a baby), confirming Chatters's initial gender determination based on the skull.

Again, Chatters turned his flashlight toward the water. Almost immediately, he saw a couple of vertebrae, bones that form the spinal column. Then he saw leg and arm bones and pieces of ribs. At that point, Chatters took off his shoes and walked barefoot into the shallow water—"so I could feel with my feet," he explained. Slowly and gently, he slid his feet

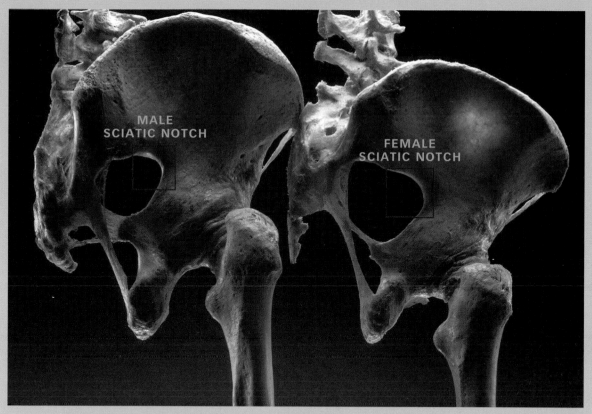

This notch, called a sciatic notch, helps anthropologists determine the gender of remains. A male *(left)* has a more acute sciatic notch than a female *(right)*.

through the mud on the bottom of the river. Shuffling this way enabled him to find objects without stepping on them. Within seconds, Chatters began picking up bones and handing them to Floyd Johnson, identifying each piece as he did so. To prevent the bones from possible damage, each piece was placed into a separate plastic bag. Continuing along the river bottom, Chatters found a cheekbone and part of the mandible.

Even as he collected these bones, Chatters grappled with the puzzle of where the bones had originally rested. Had they been buried far away and simply washed downstream? Or had they fallen out of the riverbank nearby, as the rising water eroded the soil?

Chatters found still more bones: another piece of the mandible and then a piece of a femur. Finding a femur is important. Potentially, a femur can offer a great deal of information about the individual to whom it belonged, including height, weight, and whether the person was active or not. A white gleam beside the fragment of femur turned out to be the bone handle of a knife. Had the person been stabbed? At this point in the investigation, there was no way to tell if the bones and the knife were associated. Even though the jumble of bones spoke against the skeleton being in situ, Chatters knew the bone-handled knife, should it date to the same time period as the remains, might help establish a cultural connection. He put the knife in a plastic bag for later examination and consideration.

Despite the dark, the team searched on. "The reason we did was because the area is a public park. The *Tri-City Herald* had already been informed about the discovery and there was going to be a story in the morning paper. We figured there might be folks who would come looking, so we wanted to pick up every bone we could find before we left," Chatters said. No one wanted any of the man's remains to become illicit souvenirs. Night finally halted the search, but Chatters planned to return when daylight and time permitted.

During the ride back to his house, Chatters and Johnson discussed the remains. Both men felt certain they were fairly old. Knowing the skull did not look Native American, Chatters wondered if the man might have been an early settler. The first European explorers who reached the area were Lewis and Clark during their 1805 expedition. Settlers of European ancestry arrived in later decades, but Chatters wasn't ready to classify the remains as of European ancestry until he'd examined the bones more thoroughly.

Later, after Johnson left, Chatters placed the plastic bags containing the bones on a table in his laboratory. He opened the bags slightly to allow the bones to dry slowly, so they wouldn't crack. Perhaps a closer look in the morning would reveal something new.

Perplexing Ancestry

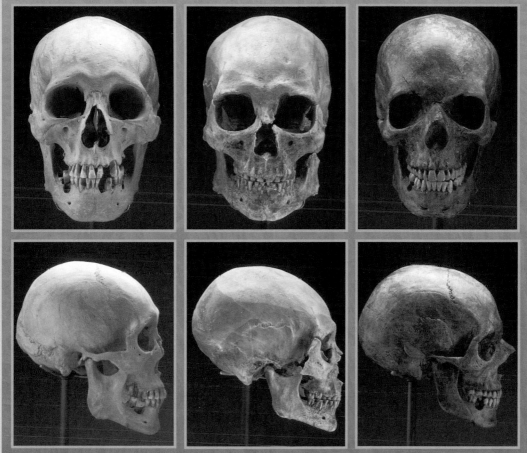

If you study the cast of the mystery man's skull *(top row, center)*, you'll understand why James Chatters didn't want to draw a hasty conclusion about the man's ancestry.

- His cheekbones are broader than the European skull *(top row, right)*, but not as broad as those of the Asian skull *(top row, left)*, which because of their shared ancient ancestry has many features similar to those found in Native American skulls.
- The width and height of the upper portion of the mystery man's skull are more similar to the European skull than the broader Asian skull.
- Depending on which area of the jaw and chin you look at *(bottom row)*, the mystery man shares similarities with both of the other skulls. The back of his jaw is somewhat robust, like the Asian's jaw, while his chin is slightly more petite, like the European's chin.

Hopefully, further study would offer more clues about who the man and his ancestors might be.

CHAPTER TWO

The Mystery DEEPENS

THE NEXT MORNING, CHATTERS GENTLY BRUSHED DRIED MUD FROM THE MAN'S CRANIUM AND FROM HIS ARM AND LEG BONES. As he had the evening before, Chatters noticed the hardened sediment stuck like small globs of oatmeal to the bones. This lumpy crust is called concretion, and it did not brush off. Chatters recognized the concretion as calcium carbonate, a naturally occurring chemical compound. Shells and certain rocks are made of calcium carbonate. Chatters was surprised to find it in Columbia Park. "We don't usually see calcium carbonate in that stretch of the river," he explained.

Next, Chatters decided to remove a small amount of concretion from one of the bones. Archaeologists often remove sediment from artifacts with a metal dental pick. In this case, that was not an option. Picking off the concretion with the instrument's sharp point would have flaked off some of the bone's outer layer as well. Chatters

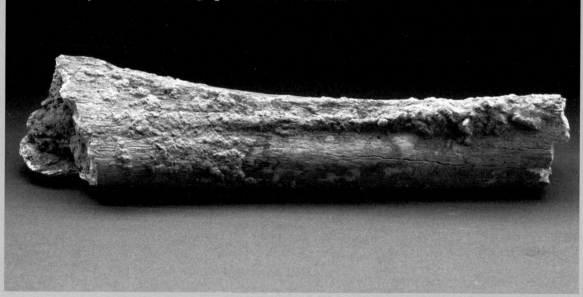

Grainy concretion made of calcium carbonate partially covered many of the bones, including this section of a femur.

avoided this by removing the calcium carbonate with simple rice vinegar from his kitchen. While removing a particle of concretion, he noticed something perplexing. Chatters described the moment:

> As I cleared a place on the right ilium, [a part of] one of the large pelvic bones, I found a hard, gray object stuck inside the bone. The object was barely visible because both it and the bone were still encrusted with concretion. I started asking myself what the object could be. Was this someone who'd been in a mining accident and had a stone embedded in his pelvis? Could it be corroded lead? Might the man have been a Civil War soldier who had shrapnel stuck in his bone? This really deepened the mystery of the man.

The skeleton seemed to be establishing a pattern: regardless of what you *think* you are looking for, don't close your eyes to other possibilities. Go to a boat race, find a skeleton. Examine a pelvic bone, find a . . . stone? Chatters wasn't sure what he was looking at. The concretion on that portion of the ilium proved stubbornly resistant to the vinegar.

Chatters realized he needed more sophisticated instruments than he had in his lab. When something embedded in a bone baffles a coroner or an anthropologist, an X-ray or a CT scan is often the next step. The radiology department at Kennewick General Hospital agreed to help.

In one way, the Kennewick remains are like a mystery novel or a TV crime show: Someone finds a dead body—usually unexpectedly. Mysterious circumstances surround the death. Crime-scene scientists arrive on the scene and quickly find clues. Scientific investigation in reality does have one important difference, though, from its fictional counterparts: it almost never follows the rules of TV pacing. There was no immediate result for Chatters. After the X-ray proved inconclusive, Chatters requested a CT scan. But a bone takes a back seat to living people when it comes to scheduling a CT scan. Chatters had to wait three days until he found out what was in the bone.

Even if the wait would have made for bad television, the results were more than worthwhile. After piecing together information from the scans, Chatters knew the object was a stone spearpoint. Things suddenly got very interesting.

How old?

Had the projectile in the bone been a bullet, forensic experts could have used ballistic fingerprinting to identify the gun that fired it. If you've ever watched a crime-scene investigation show, you've probably seen ballistic fingerprinting in action. Every gun barrel leaves marks on the soft metal used in bullets. The markings on a bullet can be used to match it to an individual weapon. This information can make a big difference in solving a case.

When ancient human remains are found with a stone projectile embedded in the bone, the process isn't much different, except instead of matching types of guns, scientists use the style and crafting technologies of stone spearpoints and arrowheads to identify who made them and when. Chatters hoped to identify the point stuck in the ilium.

The point was thin, long, and broad—similar to the shape of a leaf from a willow tree. The tip was broken, probably by the impact of hitting the bone. Taking this into account, Chatters estimated the length of the point had been 2¾ inches (7 centimeters). Chatters had seen points like this one and believed it belonged to a group of points called Cascade points. In the northwestern Pacific area, prehistoric hunters made Cascade points five thousand to nine thousand years ago. This also gave Chatters another bit of information: because of its age, the point had

CT Scanning

A special scanner that uses a technology known as computed tomography can create a three-dimensional image of an object. If you've ever watched a hospital drama on TV, you've heard of it—they typically call it a CT scan. Doctors use this scan to create images of tumors and other internal medical conditions not easily observed from the outside. Unlike a regular X-ray machine, a CT scanner creates a large number of digital images, called slices, of an object. Each slice is taken from a slightly different position and contains hundreds of digital measurements.

CT scanning is a technology that isn't standing still. In its early days, information from each slice had to be pieced together with the others to create an image. Today, new software programs plot the measurements from individual slices into points on a three-dimensional grid. The programs combine all the slices and create a three-dimensional image that can be manipulated in ways that permit all sides of the object—and even its internal structure—to be studied. Scientists use these improved programs to revisit and explore objects in ways that were impossible fifteen years ago.

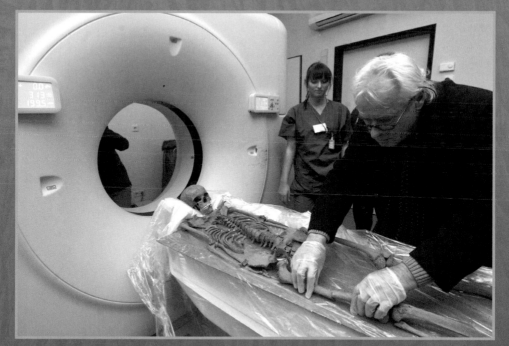

A scientist positions a six-thousand- to seven-thousand-year-old female skeleton from the Museum for Natural History and Prehistory in Dessau, Germany, prior to scanning with a hospital CT scanner.

likely been attached to a spear or a slender dart that was several feet long, not to an arrow. Bows and arrows were not introduced into the Columbia River basin region until twenty-three hundred years ago.

Finding the point embedded in the man's ilium changed everything. It practically ruled out the possibility that the remains were those of a European settler. In fact, the odds seemed high they belonged to someone who had lived thousands of years ago. Yet the skull's appearance was not like those of Native Americans.

By this time, Chatters had asked Catherine MacMillan, a physical anthropologist at Central Washington University, to evaluate the skeleton. Based on the shape of the skull and the shape of the teeth, she was convinced the man was not an Indian. Chatters was in a quandary. "I felt this could be an amazing, really important scientific discovery. We don't have the remains of any people from the early Cascade period. And to have someone with a spearpoint in him—that means interpersonal violence. That's a record of a different kind," Chatters explained.

James Chatters believed the stone embedded in the pelvic bone was a Cascade point, like the one shown below.

STUMBLING ON PREHISTORY

Identifying the spearpoint made an already puzzling mystery even more intriguing. Dating the bones was the next logical step. Chatters contacted Floyd Johnson who, as coroner, had the authority to approve sending a metacarpal—specifically the fifth metacarpal from the individual's left hand, the one that connects the pinkie finger to the wrist—to the University of California–Riverside. There, scientists would prepare the bone so it could supply a date, called a radiocarbon date, which would determine how old the remains were. However, Chatters would have to wait, yet again, for laboratory confirmation of what the physical evidence before him indicated: that the skeleton was a significant scientific find—maybe even a prehistoric one.

It's hard to believe that Thomas and Deacy's spur-of-the moment decision to watch a boat race by wading in a river could lead to a monumental scientific discovery, but archaeology often follows unexpected paths. More than fifty years earlier, another spur-of-the-moment change in plans unearthed a mummy in Nevada.

THE MUMMY IN SPIRIT CAVE

North America's oldest mummy had been a slight man, scarcely 5 feet 4 inches (1.6 m) tall and 135 pounds (61 kilograms). In his early forties at the time of his death, he was a respected, older member of the community. They'd almost lost him several months before, when something fractured his skull. During the fall and winter months since then, his injury had slowly continued healing. Recently, however, he hadn't been well. This time it was more serious than the usual twinges that plagued his lower back. This time four of his teeth had been giving him a lot of trouble. At times, they made his mouth hurt with a fierce ache. Chewing food pained him. And sometimes pus drained from the base of the teeth. Each day he grew weaker, feeling worse all the time. Hungry, he managed to swallow a meal of small fish. But by that time, even nutritious food could not make him well. A few hours later, the man died. While he would be missed, no one had liked seeing him in pain. Now, at least, his suffering had ended.

Those who cared about him laid his body on a rabbit fur blanket. Well-worn hide moccasins were on his feet. His breechcloth, made of plant fibers, was tied around his waist. Placing him on his side, the person preparing his body bent the man's knees up toward his chest and his right arm upward at the elbow, nestling his hand beneath his chin. His left arm lay draped across his pelvis. When this was done, the soft, fur blanket was wrapped closely around his body. The man's blanketed remains were placed on two woven mats. The one around the upper half of his body was folded in two, providing an added measure of protection for his head and chest. Finally, a large mat made of tule, a long reedlike plant that grew in the marshes nearby, was wrapped around the entire bundle, its corners tied tightly at the man's feet. It was time for final good-byes.

Carefully, someone carried the man's body up to the dry, protected cave chosen for his burial. Looking outward from the cave entrance, whoever buried the man could easily see the marshes of the large lake below, teeming with the small fish that the man had often eaten. Yet the cave's mouth, scarcely more than a slit in Earth's surface, was difficult, if not impossible, to see from the surface of the lake. Rocks overhung the opening, and the floor sloped in such a way that rain and water running off the surrounding rock couldn't enter.

To avoid bumping their heads, the people who buried the man crouched as they made their way to the burial pit near the back corner. Before they lay him in his grave, someone lined the bottom and sides with sagebrush. After placing the bundle into the grave, more sagebrush was scattered over the remains along with rocks to fill in and cap the grave. Over time, the wind blew fine, dry sand into the cave further burying the man's remains.

In the years since then, many people entered the cave. Eventually, it became known as Spirit Cave. Time passed. Spirit Cave Man's family and

Though the lake that Spirit Cave once overlooked is long gone, it's easy to see why Paleoamericans thought this cave, with its unusual rock formations (*detail, inset*) and sheltered entrance, was an ideal resting place for their dead.

friends died. No one remembered the man who lay buried inside the cave. He might have remained forgotten if it hadn't been for a rattlesnake.

SNAKE!

Most people wouldn't think stumbling across a rattlesnake was lucky. Sydney Wheeler and his wife, Georgia, certainly didn't think so—at first. At the time Sydney encountered the snake, they were busily involved in the 1940 archaeological field season. Working as archaeologists for the Nevada State Parks Commission, the Wheelers explored and excavated more than twenty caves in the rocky terrain surrounding Fallon, a city in western Nevada. Today the region is arid and barren, with only spotty tussocks of grasses and plants that can tolerate the desert conditions. But twelve thousand years ago, the area was quite different. A giant lake, called Lake Lahontan, covered almost all the northwestern part of what is now Nevada. Marshlands fringed its shoreline. Here and there, caves overlooked the water.

About ten thousand years ago, the climate changed and grew warmer, spelling doom for Lake Lahontan, which slowly evaporated. Caves like Spirit Cave, once waterfront property, now occupy terraces that ring the ancient lake's empty basin.

The Wheelers traipsed up and down the terraces searching for signs of ancient occupation. And on one of those treks, Sydney came face-to-face with a rattlesnake. Although he dodged the rattlesnake's strike, doing so badly twisted his leg. The long hikes they had planned up crumbly, steep terraces were suddenly out of the question for the immediate future. Georgia, making the best of a bad situation, suggested they investigate Spirit Cave, which wasn't a long walk from the road. It turned out to be a good decision.

As they removed a 1-foot-deep (0.3 m) layer of fine sand, Georgia uncovered part of a woven tule mat and a scattering of human bones. She and Sydney packed the mat for transport to a museum but reburied the bones (designated as Burial #1) elsewhere in the cave—perhaps thinking their incomplete nature would not have great scientific value—and continued excavating. Directly beneath Burial #1, they found a layer of rocks. Beneath it were the carefully prepared remains of the man who had been buried in the sagebrush-lined grave.

The arid climate and protected environment of Spirit Cave had dried and preserved the man's remains. Human or animal bodies that have been preserved are called mummies. Mummification can be the result of artificial preservation—as in the famous Egyptian mummies. Mummification also occurs naturally when remains are subject to very cold or very dry conditions. The man buried in Spirit Cave is a partially preserved mummy formed naturally under dry conditions.

After lifting the bundle from the burial pit, the Wheelers removed the tule covering. Beneath the edges of the woven mats and the fur blanket, they glimpsed bones. They also saw what looked like mummified tissue and strands of hair. The rest of the body remained hidden from view, still protected by the woven mats and the blanket. The Wheelers brought the mummy and its coverings to the Nevada State Museum.

When objects that have been protected for a long time are exposed to a change in environmental conditions, such as temperature or sunlight, they often undergo changes. Spirit Cave Man was no exception. Chemical reactions occurred when the mummy was brought outside the cave. The tufts of hair that lay across his skull changed in color from

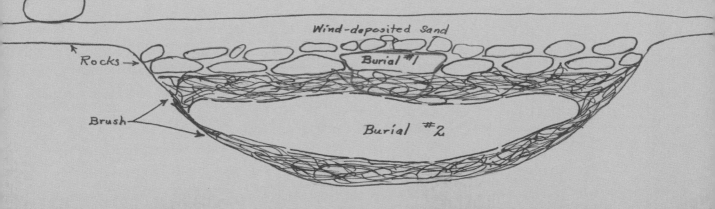

A cross section of the Spirit Cave burials as drawn by the Wheelers.

The Wheelers' photograph of Spirit Cave Man's remains in situ allows present-day archaeologists to see exactly how the burial looked as the grave was being excavated.

brownish black to reddish brown within hours. For this reason, scientists in the field must record their impressions of newly discovered remains immediately.

When anthropologists examined the mummy in the laboratory, based on 1940s archaeological knowledge, they concluded the remains were those of a young adult male—and thus he became known as Spirit Cave Man.

The anthropologists noted and described his fur blanket, fiber breechcloth, and the woven mats that had covered his body. They examined his moccasins and the antelope-skin patches sewn onto the right shoe. They noticed that woven tule lined his shoes, serving as socks to protect and cushion his feet. Based on the knowledge available at that time, they concluded he died sometime between fifteen hundred and two thousand years ago. The man's remains, his moccasins, and the mats and blanket that covered him were placed in special storage at the museum. And there he remained, silent once again, for more than fifty years. Fortunately, his silence was only temporary.

AN
Atomic
Date

James Chatters and other archaeologists don't have to rely on spearpoints for dating bones. Since the 1960s, scientists have been able to use an instrument called an accelerator mass spectrometer to analyze the amount of an element called carbon present in an object. The result of this analysis is a radiocarbon date.

All living organisms contain carbon, one of Earth's most abundant elements. A carbon atom normally contains six protons and six neutrons in its nucleus. But sometimes the number of neutrons in an atom varies. Each variation is called an isotope. Carbon has three naturally occurring isotopes. Two of them are stable, but one, carbon-14, is not.

It is radioactive and decays. And that's what makes it useful as a dating tool.

Plants absorb carbon-14 during photosynthesis, the process that creates life-sustaining nutrients from carbon dioxide gas, water, and sunlight. Animals, including humans, take in carbon-14 when they eat green plants or the meat of an animal that has eaten them. While an organism lives, it continuously replenishes the amount of carbon-14 in its cells. When an organism dies, it no longer takes in carbon-14. It takes 5,730 years for half—50 percent—of the carbon-14 contained in an organism's remains to disappear. In double that time—11,460 years—half of the remaining amount of carbon-14 decays. At that point, only 25 percent of the original amount of carbon-14 is left. By the time 50,000 years has passed since the plant or animal died, the amount of carbon-14 still remaining is so small that it's not possible to measure accurately.

To find out how old a bone is scientists remove a small piece from the bone and extract a protein called collagen from it. They use scientific processes to convert the collagen into pure carbon. After that, the sample is placed into an accelerator mass spectrometer, where it is bombarded by a special kind of particle. This causes the

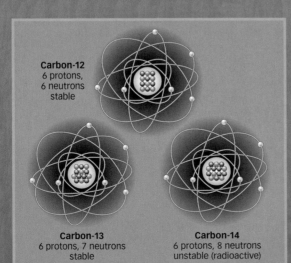

Carbon-12
6 protons,
6 neutrons
stable

Carbon-13
6 protons, 7 neutrons
stable

Carbon-14
6 protons, 8 neutrons
unstable (radioactive)

different isotopes of carbon contained in the sample to be released. Finally, the accelerator mass spectrometer counts and averages the number of decay particles emitted by the sample's carbon-14 atoms. From this number, scientists calculate how many years ago the bone stopped absorbing carbon-14 or, in other words, how long ago the animal or the person died. A date obtained with this process is called a radiocarbon date.

Scientists can be confident the date obtained is close to how long ago the organism actually died. But like any series of measurements, variations occur. "Think of measuring a table ten times. If each measurement is done to a precision of 1/100th of an inch [0.25 millimeters], you'll probably get ten slightly different numbers. The table's actual measurement falls within the range of those numbers. A radiocarbon date is no different," explained geologist Thomas Stafford, an expert in radiocarbon dating. For this reason, a radiocarbon date always includes the mathematical symbol ±, which means "plus or minus." It tells people how much the object's age may vary from the radiocarbon date. "The range of years narrows each time new technology improves the instrumentation," Stafford added.

Radiocarbon dating provides an excellent example of why it is important to reevaluate information as new knowledge becomes available. At first, scientists believed the amount of carbon-14 in Earth's atmosphere and oceans was always the same. We now know this is not true. Earth's carbon-14 content has risen and fallen several times during the past forty thousand years. During these periods, living organisms absorbed more or less carbon-14 according to the amount present in the atmosphere at that time. This must be taken into account when radiocarbon dating an object, or the calculated age will indicate the object is younger or older than it truly is. (Remember, the spectrometer obtains a date by measuring the amount of carbon-14 in the sample.) But how were scientists to know when and how long ago those periods occurred?

Information obtained from the growth layers found in trees and reef-building organisms called corals plus carbon-14 from the annual ice layers found in very deep ice in Antarctica has helped scientists identify when fluctuations in Earth's carbon-14 levels occurred. Based on this information, mathematical equations calibrate, or correct, for the fluctuations and convert a radiocarbon date into accurate calendar years. All the skeletal ages in this book have been determined by radiocarbon dating. However, for ease of interpretation, the ages have been calibrated to calendar years.

Georgia and Sydney Wheeler transported Spirit Cave Man's remains to the museum taking care not to dislodge the two woven mats that covered and protected them.

ANCIENT!

Fifty years after Spirit Cave Man was discovered, the story of Kennewick Man—as many people had started calling him—was speeding up. On August 26, 1996, official radiocarbon dating results from the laboratory at the University of California–Riverside arrived in Floyd Johnson's office and pulled the rug from beneath everyone's feet. Kennewick Man's hand bone was 9,415 to 9,490 years old!

The bones were a lot older than anyone had suspected. Kennewick Man was a Paleoamerican. The prefix *paleo* means "ancient." In this book, the term *Paleoamerican* refers to human remains older than eight thousand years. As one of the most complete sets of Paleoamerican remains ever found in the United States, the truly ancient man became even more important. At this point, the metal knife found near the skeleton became irrelevant. Its age was less than a couple of hundred years—thousands of years younger than the bones.

Kennewick Man's story was rapidly changing from a local crime-scene drama into something much larger and more profound.

SOMETIMES TWO EQUALS ONE

Not far from Spirit Cave Man's grave, at the bottom of an excavated trench, the Wheelers found two woven bags, one on top of the other. One bag contained a smaller bag inside it. This bag and the other bag contained cremated human remains. Because no soil lay between the bags, the Wheelers concluded the bags were buried together, at the same time. They assumed each bag contained the remains of one person. Fifty-four years later, radiocarbon dating determined the cremations were about 375 years younger than Spirit Cave Man.

In 1996 physical anthropologists scrutinized the many, small charred bones and realized a number of the bone fragments in one bag fit perfectly together with fragments from the other bag—the femurs being just one example. Matching the fragments' color, char patterns, and broken edges helped them reassemble the skeleton. Partially based on the skeleton's size, they concluded the remains contained in both bags belonged to the same person—a young woman who was eighteen to twenty-two years old when she died. Reexamination certainly can lead to eyebrow-raising news!

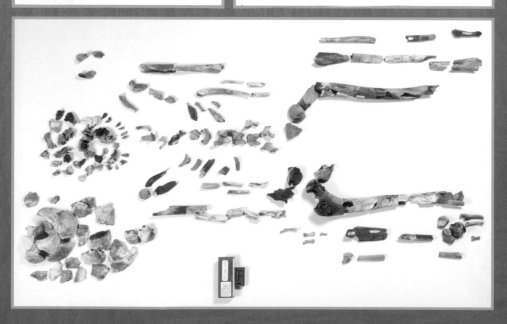

CHAPTER THREE

The StAkeS

UP TO THIS MOMENT, THE STORY OF THE
BONES FOUND IN THE COLUMBIA RIVER
UNFOLDED IN A FAIRLY PREDICTABLE MANNER.
People find unidentified human remains and law
enforcement officials seek to identify them about
forty-four hundred times every year in the United
States. In the vast majority of cases, the story ends
with identification of the deceased and perhaps
notification of next of kin. Every so often, though,
a case takes an unexpected turn and develops
into a much more dramatic situation—an unsolved
murder, for example. But only the most exceptional
cases become part of an epic story that's been
unfolding in the scientific community for decades—
one whose final chapters might hold answers to
questions much larger than how did those bones
get in the river.

HOW DID WE GET HERE?

At around nine thousand years old, Kennewick Man is ancient, but he isn't even close to being one of the earliest humans. Human fossils many thousands of years old have been found in Africa, Asia, Europe, and Australia. The oldest ones are in Africa, and they are 195,000 years old. This supports the theory that humankind originated in Africa and then wandered away and settled other continents. A number of hypotheses developed in the first half of the twentieth century to explain the movements of humanity's earliest ancestors, including how people spread into the New World. Might Kennewick Man, whose skull is so unlike those of recent Native Americans, offer clues about North America's paleosettlers?

THE TIP OF THE SPEAR

In the early 1960s, a model, or scientific explanation, called Clovis-first, attempted to explain how people arrived in the New World. Stone spearpoints supplied the evidence. Thirty years earlier, at excavations near Clovis, New Mexico, archaeologists unearthed some distinctive

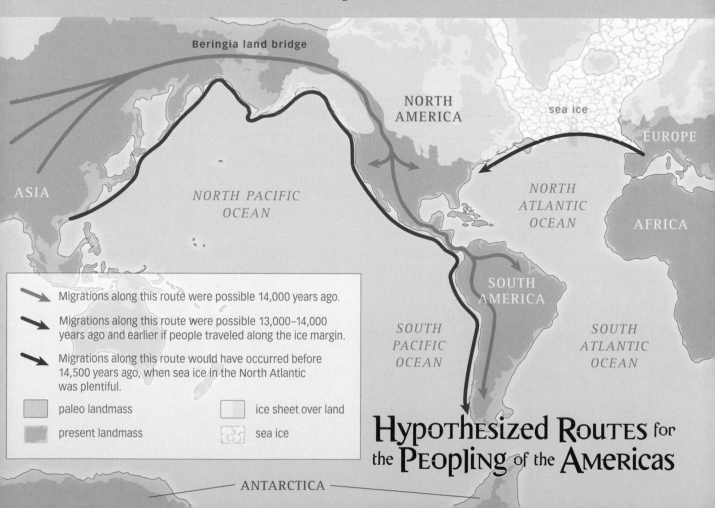

Beringia land bridge

NORTH AMERICA

sea ice

EUROPE

ASIA

NORTH PACIFIC OCEAN

NORTH ATLANTIC OCEAN

AFRICA

SOUTH AMERICA

SOUTH PACIFIC OCEAN

SOUTH ATLANTIC OCEAN

Migrations along this route were possible 14,000 years ago.

Migrations along this route were possible 13,000–14,000 years ago and earlier if people traveled along the ice margin.

Migrations along this route would have occurred before 14,500 years ago, when sea ice in the North Atlantic was plentiful.

paleo landmass

present landmass

ice sheet over land

sea ice

Hypothesized Routes for the Peopling of the Americas

ANTARCTICA

spearpoints. Since then, Clovis points, as they became known, have been found in nearly every state of the continental United States and have been dated as 12,800 to 13,250 years old.

Because no artifacts older than Clovis had been discovered, anthropologists concluded the Clovis people were the first humans to arrive in the New World. The Clovis-first model postulates an initial wave of big-game hunters crossed from Asia into what is now Alaska via the Beringia land bridge. Subsequent generations traveled southward, into all areas of the New World, through an ice-free corridor that existed between present-day Canadian provinces of British Columbia and Alberta.

However, the discovery of new Paleoamerican sites, some of which *predate* Clovis by at least two thousand to three thousand years, has led many scientists to seek explanations other than Clovis-first.

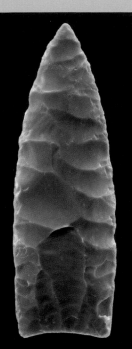

Clovis points like this one have been found throughout North America.

BY BOAT

If not Clovis-first, then what? More recent models suggest people arrived in the New World in multiple waves. In addition to crossing the Beringia land bridge, these models hypothesize that Paleoamericans arrived in boats. Recent research indicates parts of the coast of Alaska were ice-free by thirteen thousand years ago. Ice-free land was available for rest stops. After passing the coast of Beringia, paleotravelers could have paddled southward, along the Pacific coast of North America.

Unfortunately, preserved paleoboats are rarer than skeletons because the materials used to build the crafts—wood and animal skins—decompose easily. More importantly, all of North America's paleocoastlines are completely submerged due to the worldwide rise in sea level as glaciers melted at the end of the Ice Age. Any existing boat remains are buried beneath ocean mud. It would take a lot more than a boat race and a dam to reveal them.

There is evidence to support the theory that paleotravelers ventured along North America's southern Pacific coast, though. In 1959 archaeologist Phil Orr discovered human bones buried 30 feet (9 m) below the ground surface, in a wall of Arlington Canyon on Santa Rosa Island off the coast of California. He identified the remains as those of a male, who he thought had lived about 10,000 years ago. About 30 years later, in 1989, reevaluation of the bones, specifically their slender nature, led anthropologists to reclassify them as belonging to a woman. She came to be known as Arlington Springs Woman. Radiocarbon testing at that time determined she died between 12,930 and 12,698 years ago, far older than Orr's estimate. This skeleton is now the oldest, directly dated set of human remains in the New World, and being found on the coast seems to provide evidence of at least coastal travel, if not migration.

The story of the Arlington Springs remains is not over. More skeletons have been found on Santa Rosa Island. Anthropologist Patricia Lambert

Archaeologists photographed Arlington Springs Man's femur before they removed it from the wall of Arlington Canyon.

noticed other skeletons that were found on the island and known to be male were gracile, or slender—a characteristic typically associated with female skeletons. Lambert alerted anthropologist John R. Johnson, curator at the Santa Barbara Museum of Natural History in California. In light of the new information, Johnson took another look at the data. "We are back to calling the remains 'Arlington Springs Man,'" Johnson concluded (for now).

CROSSING ATLANTIC ICE

In 1999 archaeologists Dennis Stanford and Bruce Bradley proposed a model theorizing that some paleotravelers arrived on the eastern coast of North America, traveling along sea ice by boat from Europe. From twenty-five thousand to fifteen thousand years ago, the Arctic Sea was widely frozen, and in much the same way people migrated from Asia along the Pacific coast, marine hunters could have traveled along the ice across the northern Atlantic Ocean and spread southward down North America's Atlantic coast, using skills similar to those used by modern Inuit people.

Is there evidence for this? Stanford and Bradley, experts on stone artifacts, think so. Stone tools and points that predate Clovis have been found along the Atlantic coast. They bear a striking resemblance to those made by people of the Solutrean culture who lived twenty thousand to sixteen thousand years ago in the region where France, Spain, and Portugal are located today. Solutrean and Clovis points have the same general shape, and the blades of certain Solutrean and Clovis tools were both formed using similar stone-chipping techniques not used by other cultures. Might a splinter Solutrean group have climbed into boats and coast-hopped westward? Might those people or their descendants have given rise to Clovis technology or influenced it? (Clovis artifacts are far more abundant on North America's eastern coast than they are in the Midwest or western parts of the continent.) So far, no Paleoamerican skeletons have been found along the North Atlantic route, not surprising since the route is submerged by hundreds of feet of water. But if one were, it would make front-page news, just like Kennewick Man. Even if no remains can be found, Paleoamericans who lived along North America's Atlantic coast have left tantalizing clues that predate Clovis, and they can't be ignored.

The banded rhyolite knife netted by the *Cinmar* in 1970 is the length of an adult human hand.

AN UNLIKELY CATCH

One day in 1970, Captain Thurston Shawn steered the ship *Cinmar* out onto the continental shelf, 46 miles (74 km) off the coast of Virginia. Fishing for scallops, his crew dropped *Cinmar*'s dredger mesh into 240 feet (73 m) of water. Uncharacteristically, within minutes of reaching the seafloor, the net became so heavy they had to reel it in. When they spilled the catch onto the deck, the crew was astonished to see a massive skull, complete with tusks and teeth. Instead of scallops, they'd caught a mastodon, an extinct member of the elephant family! Rinsing mud from the pile of bones revealed an even more surprising treasure: a 7½-inch-long (19 cm) stone knife in perfect condition. Captain Shawn loaned part of a tusk, a molar, and the knife to the Gywnn's Island Museum, in Virginia.

In 2008—almost forty years later—geologist Darrin Lowery saw the specimens and brought them to the attention of Dennis Stanford for further examination. Scientific tests on the knife indicate it is made of an igneous rock called rhyolite taken from a source in present-day southern Pennsylvania or northern Maryland.

This is a piece of the mastodon tusk that the dredger scooped up with the *Cinmar* knife blade.

Radiocarbon dating for the mastodon tusk determined it was 22,500 to 23,000 years old. Since the two items were discovered together in one scoop—presumably in situ on the seafloor—an association between the two, although not proven, seems likely. In fact, Stanford believes someone used the Cinmar knife to butcher the mastodon after it was killed.

The Cinmar knife and other similar knives found along the mid-Atlantic seacoast are generating a lot of discussion and, at times, heated debate. Based on sea-level evidence, the last time the Cinmar site was a terrestrial, or land, environment was 14,000 to 14,500 years ago—definitely pre-Clovis. The discovery of the Cinmar knife and many other stone tools along the eastern coast and in the offshore waters of the United States provides rock-hard evidence (pun intended) that Paleoamericans were there.

Questions no less monumental than how did we get here are at stake whenever Paleoamerican remains and artifacts are found. Each individual has a story to tell. Would Kennewick Man tell his?

BACK TO SPIRIT CAVE

As you might have noticed, the story you read earlier about Spirit Cave Man's final months would not have been possible based on the Wheeler's initial examination of the mummy. In fact, when they found Spirit Cave Man, the term *Paleoamerican* hadn't even been coined. Fortunately, the Wheelers' initial examination was not the last.

In 1994 Nevada State Museum curator Amy Dansie sent samples from Spirit Cave to the University of California–Riverside for radiocarbon dating—a technology that had been unavailable to the Wheelers. "When Donna Kirner called me from the laboratory with the results, she said, 'Are you sitting down? One of your individuals is very old,'" Dansie recalled. The news Spirit Cave Man's mummy was 10,550 to 10,750 years old stunned her. "It took several days to sink in just how old—older than civilization, basically." The news skyrocketed him to fame as America's oldest mummy.

In mid-July 1996, a research team that included forensic anthropologists Doug Owsley and Richard Jantz examined Spirit Cave Man with technologies and knowledge unavailable in the 1940s. Their investigations provided a new understanding and appreciation of the man and his life.

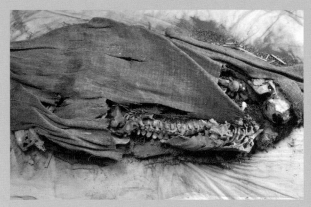

The identification of the type of weave used to make the inner woven mat surprised everyone. Spirit Cave Man's spine is visible along the mat's edge.

The inner mat closely draped Spirit Cave Man's skull. Tufts of well-preserved hair offered information about his hairstyle.

By examining the materials found in Spirit Cave Man's abdominal region, scientists could determine the content of his last meal.

Hairstyles have long been a source of identifying information. If a police officer needs to describe a missing person, it's a safe bet that hair color and length will be among the first items in a list of features. How might a Paleoamerican have chosen to wear his or her hair? Not surprisingly, preserved Paleoamerican human hair is even rarer than bone. So the tufts of hair still clinging to Spirit Cave Man's skull tell us something about paleo hair fashions. Strands of his hair measured from 6 to nearly 8 inches long (19 to 20 cm). The ends of some of the strands were cut at an angle. A blade of some sort was used to give him a chin-to shoulder-length hairstyle.

Knowing what a Paleoamerican ate for his or her last meal on Earth is as rare as knowing the hairstyle. Yet Spirit Cave Man told the anthropologists exactly what he had eaten. As Owsley and Jantz probed the mummy's abdominal area, they found dried feces. Biologist L. Kyle Napton further investigated and identified the fecal matter. Microscopic examination revealed Spirit Cave Man had eaten minnows hours before he died. The examination also found pollen from pine trees. Since this type of pollen forms in the spring, its presence indicates Spirit Cave Man died in spring or very early summer.

Unlike most prehistoric people, Spirit Cave Man had all thirty-two teeth when he died, but five had fallen out after his death. (The research team knew this by the appearance of his tooth sockets.) Perhaps they are still somewhere in the cave. Unfortunately for Spirit Cave Man, three molars had been actively abscessing, or infected and containing pus, at the time of death. These were no minor toothaches. His teeth were worn to the point where the pulp chambers of the teeth were exposed. Harmful bacteria entered his body and caused infection, which led to abscessing. The bacteria would have passed into Spirit Cave Man's blood, which spread the infection throughout his body. The infection related to Spirit Cave Man's abscessed teeth may have led to his death.

Spirit Cave Man's bones continued the tale. First, reexamination of his skull and pelvic bones led to a revision of his age from the 1940s estimate that he was a young adult. The revised age—forty to forty-four years—made him an elder of the community.

Notably, his spine had thirty-five vertebrae, one more than usual for the human spine. Having an extra vertebra may be passed on genetically. It's not a birth defect that would have caused Spirit Cave Man severe problems, but in conjunction with minor arthritis and a few herniated discs in several of his vertebrae, he probably would have had an achy back.

He was no stranger to pain. At some point, Spirit Cave Man had fractured his right hand, but the break had completely healed. Several months before his death, Spirit Cave Man suffered a far more serious injury. Like Kennewick Man, it seemed possible that Spirit Cave Man had known violence in his life. His skull had been fractured in the area just behind his left eye. Fractures radiating from the injury site, which was about the size of a nickel, were similar in pattern to the breaks caused by a blow, possibly from another person. Had Spirit Cave Man been in a fight? Had someone hit him on the head, perhaps with a rock, intending to kill him?

Beyond the skull fracture, it was the overall shape of Spirit Cave Man's skull that surprised Owsley. It is very different from the thousands of Native American skulls Owsley has examined, including those of the Paiute and Shoshone, tribes that still live in the area. He decided he had to look at other Paleoamerican skulls to see if they were different too.

Spirit Cave Man's remains weren't the only source of new information. The woven mats wrapped around his remains were a big surprise. When Amy Dansie looked closely at the two inner mats, she realized Sydney Wheeler had misidentified the pattern used to weave them. He referred to them as "twined" mats. They actually were a pattern called diamond plaiting.

The weaving patterns used by different tribes are sufficiently distinct that experts can determine which group of people created a specific woven artifact. This is extremely important when trying to determine cultural affiliation. James Adovasio, an expert on ancient American

The diamond plaiting weave used to make the inner mats found in Spirit Cave is clear in this close-up. The Ainu people of ancient Japan also used this technique.

textiles, examined the Spirit Cave mats. "They are woven differently than the way inhabitants in that region have produced their baskets during the past 2,000 years."

"Perhaps even more intriguing is the matting from Spirit Cave is almost identical to those made by the Ainu people," said Dansie. The ancient ancestors of the Ainu were a group of people who lived in the area of present-day Japan. "If he shared ancestors with the Ainu, might they have carried the same weaving technology with them as they migrated along the coast of Japan, dropping off kin there, as others continued on to America?" Heated discussion surrounds this theory, which will require more evidence to prove or disprove.

A MATTER OF RESPECT

Spirit Cave Man was given the opportunity to teach us something about his people and life in Paleoamerica. Unfortunately, before Kennewick Man could say his piece and contribute to the Paleoamerican tale in a similar way, he would have a role in a different and no less complicated story, one affected by decades of disrespect and indignity.

Scientists like the Wheelers, who followed the best archaeological guidelines of their day, and unintentional discoverers like Thomas and Deacy, who reported their find to the authorities, are not the only ones who have turned up bones—far from it. Not every discoverer has acted with respect for the dignity of the remains they have uncovered. Unfortunately, finding a record of these crimes is depressingly easy:

> *An Indian skeleton was unearthed at Kirkland [Illinois] the other*
> *day, and denizens of that place are decorating the bones for parlor*
> *ornaments.*

This excerpt from an article from 1886 appeared in the Looking Back column of author Sally Walker's local paper while she was working on the early drafts of this book. This record of disrespect for ancient remains was literally delivered to her doorstep.

This random news snippet from a 125-year-old newspaper says almost everything that needs to be said about why Kennewick Man's remains were destined to spend significant time in the court system. The record of treatment of Native American remains up until the last half of the twentieth century contains an appalling amount of grave desecration and looting on behalf of private collectors and public museums.

Archaeological practices have long moved away from the cultural insensitivity demonstrated in the excerpt, but the wounds to the relationship between scientists and the Native American community were numerous and haven't healed quickly.

By the end of the twentieth century, legislation finally began to address and atone for the historical mistreatment of remains. On November 16, 1990, the Native American Graves Protection and Repatriation Act (NAGPRA) became federal law, codifying procedures for returning Native American remains and cultural items to descendants and tribes.

NAGPRA quickly became an issue in Kennewick. The Umatilla tribe, who had lived in the area for many centuries, had claimed remains that had appeared on nearby Corps of Engineers-managed land in the past. Thomas and Deacy's discovery soon caught the tribe's attention. Shortly after the local newspaper reported that a skeleton had been found, the tribe requested that the Corps of Engineers give it to them without further scientific study. At that point, no one knew who should be responsible for the remains.

Many of Kennewick Man's bones—like this rib bone—were broken into several pieces. When and how they fractured was a critical question for researchers.

A CLOSER LOOK

During the month following the discovery, with the skeleton's future still in doubt, work at the site continued. Chatters, some of his colleagues, and Corps of Engineer scientists, returned to the river ten times. They gathered more bone fragments and collected soil samples from the riverbank. After their final visit to the site, having sifted through many buckets of mud, they had collected more than three hundred human and nonhuman bone fragments.

In his laboratory, Chatters had scrutinized each bone fragment. First, he determined what type of bone it was—whether it was an arm, a leg, or a rib—and then he sorted the bones accordingly. One of the first things Chatters established was the man's age at the time he died. Teeth and specific areas of certain bones gave him the evidence he needed.

An adult's third set of molars, often called wisdom teeth, erupt at about eighteen years of age. Two of Kennewick Man's third molars, one in his upper jaw and one in the lower, were still present. (The other two had been lost, one before his death, the other afterward.) Chatters concluded the man was no younger than eighteen when he died.

Kennewick Man's arm and leg bones gave Chatters more information. These bones have two main parts: the shaft—the long, straight part of the bone—and the epiphyses, the bony caps located at each end of the long bones. In children, the epiphyses connect to the shaft with cartilage, a semirigid, translucent connective tissue. As a person ages, bone replaces cartilage and the line disappears. In girls, this occurs by the age of sixteen, and in boys by about nineteen. Kennewick Man's epiphyses were completely fused—the sign of a mature adult (see photo page 48).

And Kennewick Man's cranium helped Chatters further narrow his age. During a human's growing years, fibrous joints exist between the bones of the skull. Zigzagging lines called sutures outline the edges of these joints. Growth occurs along these lines of suture and the intricate convolutions hold the cranial bones tightly together. Sutures on the skulls of young people are more visible than those on an adult's. Sometimes sutures on middle-aged and older people fuse together and even disappear. Since Kennewick Man's sutures were only faintly visible, Chatters concluded he had been thirty-five to forty-five years old when he died.

NAGPRA in Practice

NAGPRA established a procedure and rules that federal agencies, as well as all public and private museums receiving federal funds, must follow. NAGPRA identifies who may claim human remains and cultural items. It provides the avenue for Native American individuals who are directly descended from a specific deceased Native American to request the remains of that ancestor and items, such as funerary and sacred objects, belonging to him or her. It also gives certain rights of ownership and control of these same items to recognized Indian tribes and to Native Hawaiian organizations, of which there are more than seven hundred.

As of October 2011, under a separate but similar act, the Smithsonian Institution's National Museum of Natural History has offered the remains of 5,620 individuals and nearly 182,500 burial artifacts and sacred objects to their affiliated Indian tribes for repatriation.

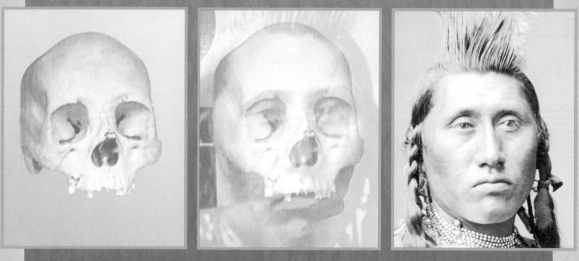

In 1994, staff at the American Museum of Natural History in New York City suspected one of the skulls in their collection was that of Chief Pretty Eagle, a respected Crow leader and warrior. At their request, Doug Owsley compared the skull with photographs of Chief Pretty Eagle and found many similarities. The photograph of Chief Pretty Eagle shows a slight asymmetry of the nose, suggesting that his nose had been broken. This is significant because the skull has a well-healed fracture of the nose. Based on cranial features, Owsley concluded the skull was the chief's. As a result, Chief Pretty Eagle's remains were returned to the Crow Nation and reinterred during a burial ceremony later that year.

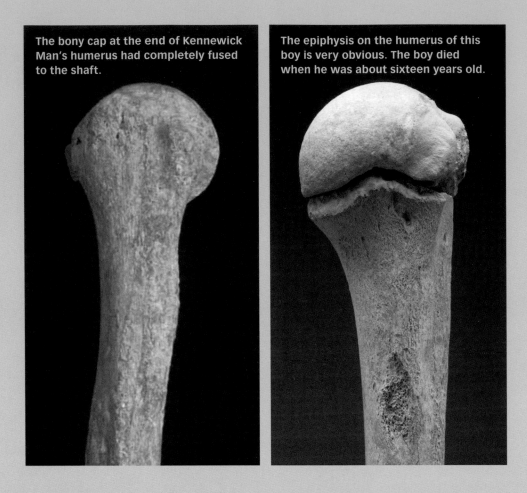

The bony cap at the end of Kennewick Man's humerus had completely fused to the shaft.

The epiphysis on the humerus of this boy is very obvious. The boy died when he was about sixteen years old.

Using certain mathematical equations that included measurements of the femurs, Chatters calculated the man was 5 feet 7 inches to 5 feet 9½ inches (1.7 to 1.8 m) tall. Chatters also used the long bones to estimate the man's weight. (Yes, determining a person's weight when alive from skeletal remains is possible.) From the results, Chatters determined the man had weighed 154 to 165 pounds (70 to 75 kg).

Chatters photographed the bones and the teeth, focusing on areas that showed possible injury or illness. One of these areas included a fracture on the man's forehead, above his left eye. Several other bones, including the ribs, showed signs of fracture prior to death. Had the man been in a fight or perhaps an accident or a fall?

After consulting a doctor, Chatters concluded the wound caused by the stone projectile point in his hip had been chronically infected. Had this caused the man a great deal of pain? When he walked, had he limped? Once again, for every answer Chatters uncovered, two more questions seemed to follow. And rumors were circulating that the Corps of Engineers was planning to give the skeleton to the Umatilla. If the skeleton was put beyond the reach of further study, there would be no answers.

When Floyd Johnson and James Chatters discussed the skeleton, they naturally wondered what the man might have looked like while alive. Creating a facial reconstruction from a skull is possible. It is occasionally done in forensic cases when authorities attempt to identify an individual. Near the end of August, Chatters made a cast, or replica, of the skull. From this, he worked with a sculptor and created a facial reconstruction of Kennewick Man. He had another motive: if the remains were ultimately given to the Umatilla—who by this time were formally requesting the remains under NAGPRA—at least he would have the copy of the skull for future reference. He also called Doug Owsley, who quickly made plans to have his research team examine Kennewick Man. Without doubt, getting to know Kennewick Man and understand his life and death was going to require a lot of rigorous, challenging, time-consuming thought. Time was one thing Chatters wasn't sure he had.

IN CUSTODY

On August 30, 1996, under orders from the Corps of Engineers, Johnson notified Chatters he was coming to take the remains. Not knowing if he—or anyone—would ever see Kennewick Man again, Chatters used the hours before Johnson's arrival to videotape the remains and take additional photos. After Johnson and a deputy arrived, they and one of Chatters's colleagues watched as Chatters put the six pieces of the femurs (each femur was broken into three pieces) and the skull inside plastic bags and placed them in a wooden box. He did the same for the rest of the bones. Finally, he screwed down the top of the box. As a final security measure, Johnson wrapped the box with yellow tape used by the sheriff's department to secure evidence. The bones were taken to the Benton County Sheriff's Office and placed in an evidence locker for safekeeping.

The controversy around the ancient remains deepened during the month of September. Owsley requested that he and other scientists be permitted to examine Kennewick Man. Meetings and discussions—some of them heated—took place among the Corps of Engineers, scientists, lawyers, and Native Americans. Everyone argued about where the remains should be stored while the legal issues were being resolved. Eventually, a member of the Colville tribe suggested they be taken to a U.S. Department of Energy laboratory in Richland, Washington, called Battelle Laboratory. The parties concerned agreed to this suggestion.

On September 10, 1996, Julie Longenecker, an archaeologist working for the Umatilla tribe, and Ray Tracy, a Corps of Engineers archaeologist who had collected some of the bones at the discovery site, opened the box containing the remains and inventoried them. Significantly, there was no record of the femurs in this inventory. Then several tribal members held a religious ceremony over the man, whom they called the Ancient One. They burned cedar twigs and scattered the ashes inside the box. In their own ways, both the scientists and the tribal leaders honored Kennewick Man's remains.

INTO THE LIMELIGHT

Meanwhile, word about the ancient skeleton spread like wildfire across the United States. To their amazement, Will Thomas and Dave Deacy, the two young men who first discovered the skull, were back in the limelight. "When I heard the news about how old the man was, I couldn't believe it. He was older than Moses, who is in the Bible!" laughed Thomas. "After that point, we gave countless interviews to newspapers and magazines. Dave and I even did two reenactments for television—one for the Discovery Channel and the other for a Korean public television channel."

Reporters called Chatters and Johnson, seeking more information and requesting photographs of Kennewick Man. Some Native Americans object to displaying photographs of Indian remains and because at that time the ancestry of the remains had not been determined, the coroner's office decided not to release photos of the remains to the news media. Instead, Chatters asked his sixteen-year-old daughter, Claire, who was studying art, to draw a picture of the man's skull. "My dad asked me to do the drawing because I had won awards for my artwork and he believed I would do a good job," Claire Chatters recalled. "I was a little nervous

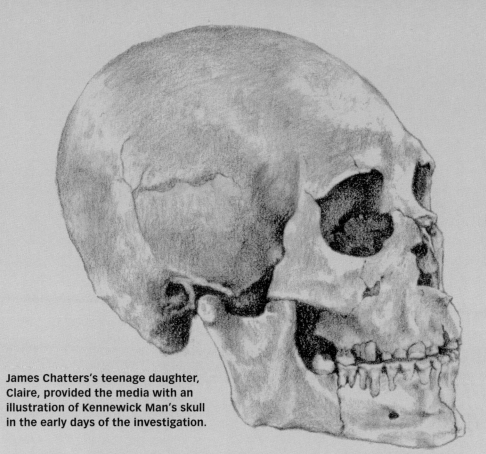

James Chatters's teenage daughter, Claire, provided the media with an illustration of Kennewick Man's skull in the early days of the investigation.

and a little excited—it was the first work I had done that was truly professional. But I remember being up for the challenge." She relied on one of her father's photographs while drawing the image. "By that time the Army Corps of Engineers had taken possession of the skeleton, so I had no choice. Because my drawing needed to be as accurate as possible, I first traced over parts of the skull in the photo. Then I drew the rest by just looking at the photo. One of the hardest parts for me was to draw the delicate little hair-line cracks where the pieces of the skull knit together [the sutures mentioned above]."

A week after the remains had been transferred to Battelle Laboratory, the *Tri-City Herald* published a legal notice stating the Army Corps of Engineers intended, under NAGPRA, to repatriate the remains to a coalition of Native American tribes consisting of the Colville, the Nez Percé, the Umatilla, the Wanapum, and the Yakama, all of whom were claiming them. Tribal oral tradition and historical documentation noted that all of these tribes had resided in the area. The date set for repatriation was October 24, 1996. It looked as if Kennewick Man's time aboveground could be under six months.

Several scientists, Doug Owsley among them, again requested the opportunity to study Kennewick Man before his bones were given for reburial. Without study, how could the Corps of Engineers know whether Kennewick Man was Native American? Also, considering how old the skeleton was, it was possible that he—even the group of people to which he belonged—might have no living descendants. And because NAGPRA states that Native American "means of, or relating to, a tribe, people, or culture that *is* indigenous to the United States . . . [emphasis added]," the law would not apply to the remains. Their requests, despite support from members of Congress, were ignored.

On October 16, 1996, after much discussion, eight scientists decided to take legal action. In the federal district court in Portland, Oregon,

THE PLAYERS IN THE KENNEWICK MAN CASE:

THE JUDGE:
Judge John Jelderks

THE PLAINTIFFS*:
Robson Bonnichsen, C. Loring Brace, George Gill, C. Vance Haynes, Richard Jantz, Douglas Owsley, Dennis Stanford, and D. Gentry Steele

THE DEFENDANTS**:
The United States of America, Department of Defense, and Army Corps of Engineers. In 2002, the U.S. Department of the Interior and the National Park Service were added as defendants, as were some employees of both departments.

OTHER PARTICIPANTS IN THE CASE:
The Confederated Tribes of the Colville, the Umatilla, and the Yakama, the Nez Percé Nation, and the Wanapum Band were not defendants in the case. They did participate in the court hearings and supplied the court with briefs, legal statements listing information, supporting evidence, and documentation that are pertinent to a case.

*A plaintiff is a person or a group who begins a lawsuit in court.
**A defendant is a person or a group who is being sued in court.

they filed a lawsuit against the United States, the Department of Defense, and the U.S. Army Corps of Engineers. And while all the scientists were anthropologists employed either by universities or by the Smithsonian Institution, they sued the government as private citizens. Their lawsuit requested the court to stop the transfer of the remains and to award the scientists the opportunity to study Kennewick Man. Members of the Indian tribes claiming the remains were not parties to the lawsuit.

One day before the date set for repatriation, Judge John Jelderks held an emergency hearing at which the Corps of Engineers agreed to postpone the transfer of the remains. Further, the court ordered the Corps of Engineers not to give the skeleton to anyone without notifying the eight scientists who were parties to the lawsuit. Kennewick Man's fate lay in the hands of the United States legal system.

A DAY IN COURT

We know that once Kennewick Man landed in the river, his story didn't quite follow the script of a TV crime show. And after Kennewick Man landed in court, things didn't move quite as quickly as they do in a TV courtroom drama, where things wrap up neatly in a single episode.

However long it would take for the court to rule on Kennewick Man's fate, the stakes were clear to all the scientists: would Kennewick Man's remains silently return to the earth, or would he add his chapter to the Paleoamerican story alongside Spirit Cave Man? And if he spoke, what might he have to say? Three more of his fellow Paleoamericans offered clues.

CHAPTER FOUR

The PaleoAmericans

MUCH LIKE KENNEWICK MAN, THE SKELETON AT ARCH LAKE REAPPEARED ONLY AFTER HUMAN ACTIVITIES ALTERED THE EARTH AROUND IT. In her case, it was construction equipment, not a river that did the earthmoving.

ON THE SHORE OF ARCH LAKE

Roads don't get built without moving dirt. When construction machinery digs through a hill, formerly hidden materials are exposed in the steep sides of a roadcut. In 1967 Gregg Moore and Cecil Clark, two amateur archaeologists, explored a roadcut in eastern New Mexico. Imagine their surprise when they found half of a human mandible. Searching farther down the slope, they discovered pieces of a human skull. Immediately, the two men notified additional members of the archaeological society to which they belonged.

The roadcut where Moore and Clark found Arch Lake Woman's remains in 1967. Her grave is in the bank of sediments found in the center right.

Further excavation by the team revealed the rest of a woman's skeleton. Since her remains were found near the area once covered by a huge lake, called Arch Lake, she has become known as Arch Lake Woman.

Unlike Kennewick Man, it was clear from the beginning that Arch Lake Woman was intentionally buried and not by an accident of nature. And of course, most of her bones were still in situ.

Although they were trained in excavation, the archaeologists realized proper examination of the burial required more expertise than they had. They decided to remove the entire burial in a large block, especially because they had noticed something that led them to think the skeleton might be really old. In the years after Arch Lake Woman's burial, new layers of undisturbed sediment were deposited on top of her grave. Those layers were similar to layers that the archaeologists had seen about 25 miles (40 km) away, which had been radiocarbon dated as more than five thousand years old. If the sediment layers covering Arch Lake Woman's grave should turn out to be the same as the distant sediment layers, her bones would have to be even older!

Arch Lake Woman was taken to Eastern New Mexico University in Portales for safekeeping. Because her remains have been well cared for during the decades since their discovery, a research team in 2000, using scientific methods and tools unavailable at the time of her discovery, was able to learn a great deal more about the young woman.

A wooden frame prevented sediment from falling away from Arch Lake Woman's remains and provided a framework for a plaster jacket.

Arch Lake Woman has shared much with us. Her skeleton is 11,640 to 11,260 years old, making her one of the oldest Paleoamericans yet found. Age indicators on her long bones, skull, and teeth revealed she was young when she died, only seventeen to nineteen years old. Measurements suggest she may have been as tall as 5 feet 5½ inches (1.7 m), quite tall when compared with other Paleoamerican women—and even taller than the average American woman today. Her weight could not be determined. Arch Lake Woman's femurs were still cemented in the sediment, so they couldn't be lifted to make the necessary measurements.

A PALEOAMERICAN TEEN

But what about Arch Lake Woman's life? Could her remains tell, for example, what kinds of food she regularly ate? Absolutely. To find the answer, scientists analyzed the collagen from a tiny piece of her femur. Our bodies manufacture collagen from the protein-rich foods, such as meat and legumes, we eat. Carbon-13 and nitrogen-15 are two of the

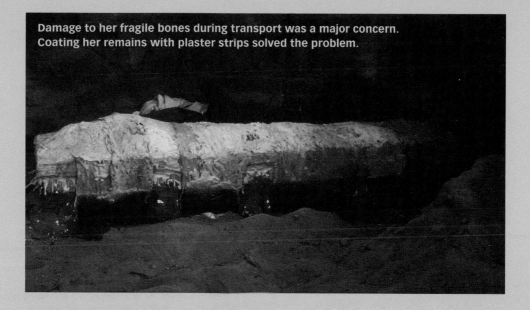

Damage to her fragile bones during transport was a major concern.
Coating her remains with plaster strips solved the problem.

stable isotopes found in collagen. They enter a person's body through
the plants and animals he or she eats. Scientists measure the stable
isotopes with an instrument called a mass spectrometer. (Although the
name is similar, it is not the same instrument as the accelerator mass
spectrometer used for radiocarbon dating). A mass spectrometer measures
and compares the amounts of carbon-13 and nitrogen-15 contained in
a sample of bone. The carbon-13 present reflects the general type of
plants a person ate, which provides information about the environment.
The amount of nitrogen-15 provides information about a person's meat
consumption—what percent of the diet was meat and whether it came
from land-dwelling animals or from fish.

Based on the results of her collagen tests, we know Arch Lake Woman
was a teen who preferred meat to vegetables. She ate both, but the isotope
results clearly showed she ate a lot more meat than plants. An extinct
species of bison were plentiful in the area where she lived, so it's likely
bison appeared on the menu often.

What kinds of activities kept Arch Lake Woman busy? Close
examination of tens of thousands of bones has taught forensic
anthropologists that the activities people do on a regular basis actually
sculpt growing bones. The muscles that enable us to move are attached
to our bones. Repeatedly using muscles for the same, strenuous chores
changes a bone's appearance. A bone responds to repeated muscle use

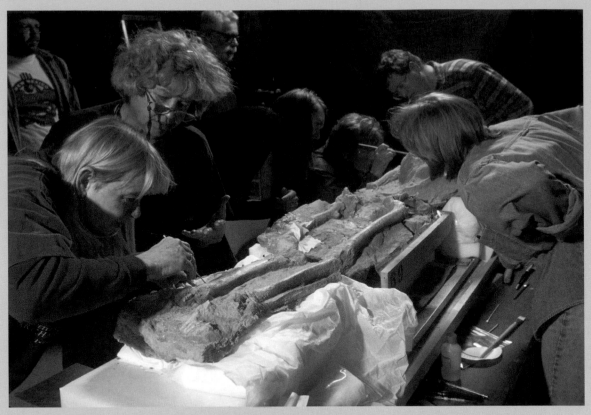

The team, including Margaret Jodry *(left)* and Doug Owsley *(background, right)*, searches for clues about Arch Lake Woman's life.

by adding more bone mass to the area where the muscles and ligaments attach to the bone. Over time, especially during the teen and young adult years, the bone becomes more robust. The diameter increases, and the ridges where the muscles are attached become more pronounced. After death, even though muscle tissue decays and disappears, the bone still tells the story of how the muscles were used.

Arch Lake Woman had robust upper arms with plenty of muscle power. She was a teen who started working hard while she was still a child. Knowing her diet was high in meat from large animals, it's likely she developed such a strong physique by working with bison hides. Preparing a hide for use as shelter, clothing, and bedding requires elbow grease. If this task occupied Arch Lake Woman's time, her arm muscles—and her bones—would show it.

Who, then, were Arch Lake Woman's companions as she toiled over a stack of hides? Who helped her pass the time as she scraped and stretched the skins? Scientists turned to her teeth for clues. Unlike Kennewick Man, Arch Lake Woman's teeth were not very worn, and so from them, it was possible to make some comparisons to other peoples. The eight teeth at the front of a person's mouth—four in the upper jaw and four in the lower—are called incisors. These are the teeth we first use when biting into an apple. Most recent Native Americans (85 to 90 percent) have incisors that exhibit a characteristic shape called shoveling. The tongue-facing surface of a shoveled incisor has a ridge along the outer edge of each side of the tooth. This gives the tooth a scoop or shovel-like appearance (see left photo on page 84). Arch Lake Woman's incisors showed only slight shoveling. Her incisors showed neither of two additional shape characteristics, called double shoveling and winging (slightly rotated upper central incisors), which are frequently found in North American Indians. Despite her teeth not resembling those of recent Native Americans, had her ancestors come from the same regions as theirs? Might she still be related in some way? And how was Arch Lake Woman related to other Paleoamericans? Unfortunately, minerals from the sediments surrounding Arch Lake Woman's skeleton had seeped into her skeleton and replaced much of the actual bone material. Her bones were too heavily mineralized for today's scientific methods to answer these questions.

A FINAL FAREWELL

We must always remember Arch Lake Woman was more than bones and teeth. Like us, she felt happiness, sadness and, perhaps, curiosity. Had she wondered about her world? What had she and her people believed about death? Did they believe in an afterlife? Her skeleton alone can't answer these questions. That's why it's so important to consider all aspects of a burial, including the position of the person's body and any grave goods. They ask us to think, to try to understand who she or he was.

The position of a body in the grave varies according to culture or circumstances of burial. Friends or relatives deliberately placed Arch Lake Woman lying on her back with her legs fully extended. People cared about her and took the time to bury her.

Arch Lake Woman wore a necklace when she was buried. Fourteen beads, made of a whitish mineral called talc, lay in an arc between her collarbones. (Later, the archaeologists found five more beads when they sifted through more sediment at the gravesite.) Talc, or rock containing it, was often used by prehistoric carvers because it is soft and can be sculpted fairly easily. Archaeologist Margaret Jodry examined the beads. "It is a privilege for me to look at her belongings. From them I try to gain a better understanding of Arch Lake Woman and her relations."

The talc beads show signs of wear, so they weren't made specifically for Arch Lake Woman's burial. Had she treasured this necklace and worn it for a long time? Had she made it herself, or had someone given it to her as a gift? While it hasn't been possible to connect her beads with a specific culture, we do know that someone believed the necklace meant something to Arch Lake Woman, important enough to bury it with her.

Meanwhile, about 500 miles (804 km) southeast of Arch Lake Woman's gravesite and as much as three hundred years later, two other Paleoamericans were laid to rest in a rockshelter in Texas.

IN THE DEPTHS OF HORN SHELTER

For thousands of years, people have considered the rockshelter overlooking the Brazos River prime real estate. Its thick rock ceiling and walls offered a safe haven for sleeping, as well as shelter from storms. The river was only a short walk away, so food and drinking water were close at hand. In short, the rockshelter was a good place to call home.

During the 1960s, amateur archaeologists Albert Redder and Frank Watt recognized this and began excavations inside the rockshelter, which became known as Horn Shelter No. 2. They dug down through almost 22 feet (6.7 m) of soil, recording every artifact and feature and in so doing learned that people had been using Horn Shelter for nearly thirteen thousand years. And then, in 1970, toward the back of the shelter, beneath nineteen slabs made of limestone, Redder and Watt found a truly remarkable grave.

TOGETHER FOREVER

The grave at Horn Shelter contained the remains of two people, both of whom died about 11,100 years ago. Using many of the same processes as those used for the examination of Arch Lake Woman,

Fifteen of the talc beads found in Arch Lake Woman's grave are shown here. Behind them is a delicately sharpened stone flake used for cutting and scraping. The tool lay near Arch Lake Woman's ribs, suggesting she may have carried it in a pouch around her waist.

Al Redder (left) describes how his team removed 22 feet (7 m) of accumulated soil from the floor of Horn Shelter No. 2. Doing so restored the shelter to its appearance as Horn Shelter Man's people would have seen it eleven thousand years ago.

scientists coaxed out their stories. The larger skeleton belonged to a man, thirty-five to forty-four years old. He stood almost 5 feet 5 inches (1.7 m) tall and weighed about 152 pounds (69 kg). His leg bones did not show signs he had regularly used them for strenuous trekking, as a hunter might, nor did his upper arm bones indicate he had regularly lifted heavy loads. The man's ulnas and radiuses, the bones in his forearms, however, were puzzling. These bones, in both of the man's arms, had unusually enlarged crests midway along their shafts (see photo page 67). The crest was more pronounced on the left radius than on the right. He also had very robust hands for a man of his size. The abnormal crests on his lower arm bones coupled with two strong hands begged further investigation. What had this man been doing?

The person who shared his grave was young—only about ten years old—and perfectly illustrates why reassessing a skeleton is important. The bones of a mature adult are fully developed. At maturity, both the pelvis and skull of a female have slightly different features than those of a male. In contrast, the bones of a child younger than mid-teens are still growing and changing. Because they haven't yet developed these distinctive features, determining whether skeletal remains are those of a boy or a girl can be difficult. Initially, scientists identified the Horn Shelter youth simply as a juvenile but likely a male. Later reexamination led to a change in this assessment. The slender bones and the small, pointed chin—both typically female features—suggest the remains are those of a girl.

Unlike Arch Lake Woman, both of the Horn Shelter people lay on their left sides, with their legs in a semiflexed position. Since the position of a body inside a grave can vary from culture to culture, it may add a link to a chain of evidence that establishes a cultural affiliation. A number of objects buried with them indicate they were buried with respect and dignity. Because fragile items decompose, Paleoamericans rarely have the opportunity to teach us something about their spiritual life or their connection with the natural world. Yet the people from Horn Shelter are doing just that. The grave goods placed with the man hint at several possibilities. Part of a turtle's shell covered his face. His head rested on top of three nested turtle shells. The young girl's head also touched them. Yet another turtle shell was placed beneath the man's left hip. It seems certain the turtle had significance to the deceased as well as to the people who buried them.

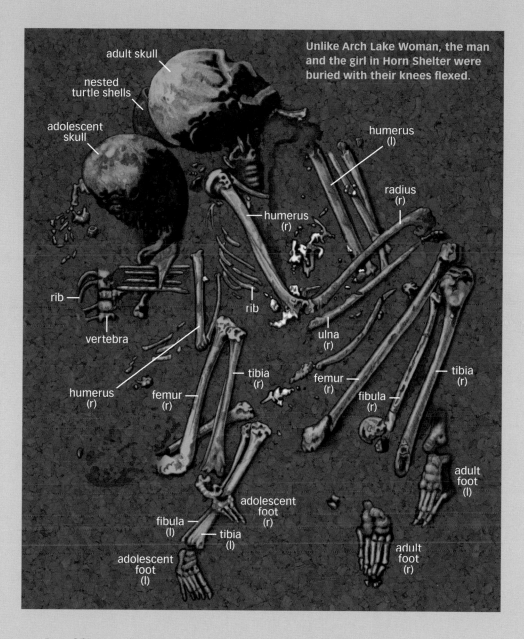

Unlike Arch Lake Woman, the man and the girl in Horn Shelter were buried with their knees flexed.

adult skull

nested turtle shells

adolescent skull

humerus (l)

radius (r)

humerus (r)

rib

rib

ulna (r)

vertebra

tibia (r)

femur (r)

tibia (r)

humerus (r)

femur (r)

fibula (r)

adult foot (l)

adolescent foot (r)

fibula (l)

tibia (l)

adult foot (r)

adolescent foot (l)

In addition, the limestone slabs capping the burial were arranged to cover both bodies while leaving the heads uncovered. Was this done to create a symbolic turtle shell for the deceased? "The turtle shells may have been a symbol of a spiritual connection. Perhaps they indicate a clan relationship shared by the man and the child, since the heads of both individuals touch the three nested turtle shells," Margaret Jodry explained.

The people who buried Horn Shelter man cradled his head on top of three nested turtle shells.

GRAVE GOODS

Additional astonishing grave goods ask us to think even more deeply about the man and girl and who they were. Claws from a badger paw and the talons of a hawk, one tucked inside his mouth, lay near the man's head. Four coyote canine teeth, with a small hole drilled through each, lay in the area of his head and neck, probably part of a necklace. The necklace's eighty-three small shell beads and one large snail shell, presumably a pendant, also raise fascinating questions. The place closest to Horn Shelter No. 2 where these shells can be found is the Gulf Coast, which is about 185 miles (300 km) downstream. Had the man received the shells from a trader who passed through the area? Had they been a gift? Or had the man walked the long distance and collected them himself? The answers to these questions are lost for now, but the man and the necklace ask us to remember his life.

For many years, a cluster of stone artifacts, located beneath the man's head led archaeologists to think he may have been a flintknapper. Stone tools, such as points, knives, and scrapers (tools used to remove flesh from bone or hide) are made from a variety of rocks, including chert and flint. Knapping is a toolmaking process that creates sharp-edged tools. A flintknapper chips progressively smaller pieces from a rock with a hammerlike tool called a billet. Two antler billets were among the tools found beneath the head of the man buried in Horn Shelter, as was a partially completed stone tool. If the man had been a toolmaker,

These shell beads were probably part of a necklace. Valued highly enough to be buried with Horn Shelter Man, we must wonder, What significance did they hold for him and his people?

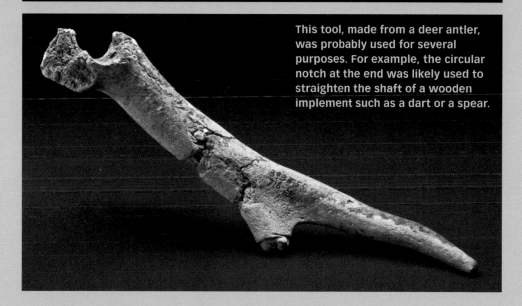

This tool, made from a deer antler, was probably used for several purposes. For example, the circular notch at the end was likely used to straighten the shaft of a wooden implement such as a dart or a spear.

he would have used his hand and arm muscles a lot, perhaps explaining his robust hands and the enlarged muscle attachment crests on his lower arm bones. Together the toolkit and bone features seemed to support the conclusion he was a toolmaker. But recently, Owsley and Jodry have begun rethinking this conclusion and replacing, or at least enriching, it with another.

Might these talons from a Swainson's hawk signify a connection between Horn Shelter Man, the sky, and his belief in a spiritual world above us?

Had Horn Shelter Man used this 2½-inch-long (6 cm) stonecutting tool in everyday life, or was it solely made for him to use in the afterlife?

For Jodry, the badger claws, shells, and hawk feet hold great significance. She wonders if Horn Shelter Man may have been a healer or a shaman. A shaman is a tribe member who connects the visible world with the spirit world. "The badger is revered for its digging ability. It can reach down into the earth where the roots of medicinal plants are. Shells are associated with water. Hawks soar above the earth, into the world above," Jodry explained. "Healers connect people with these powerful spiritual medicines." How might being a healer affect Horn Shelter Man's robust hands and lower arms? Drumming is a common part of healing ceremonies around the world. "A healer may often drum for hours, even all night. One hand holds the drum. The other hand holds the beater and rhythmically hits the drumhead. Sometimes a healing ceremony may last so long that a helper actually supports a healer's arm as she or he holds the drum so the drumming can continue." Relentless repetition like this definitely affects the hand and arm muscles. As a result of Jodry's theory, she and Owsley are talking with drummers (including native healers) as they investigate how sustained, steady, repetitive drumming affects the lower arm bones. This fascinating possibility underscores, yet again, why we must continually reexamine and, if necessary, reevaluate our conclusions. Only then can we hope to understand the lessons ancient people can teach us.

A LITTLE GIRL

You can't help but wonder about the young girl buried in Horn Shelter No. 2. Who was she? How did she die? Her relationship, if any, to the man remains a mystery. She might have been a family member. If the man had been a healer, perhaps she was his

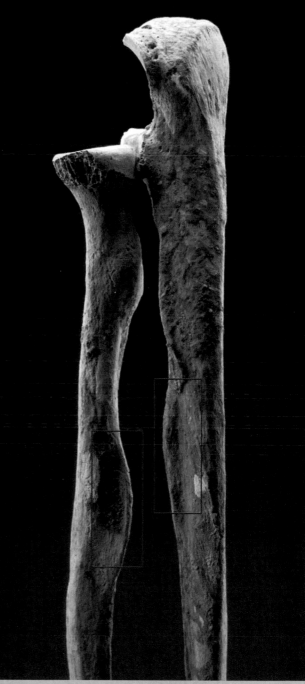

Enlarged crests on Horn Shelter Man's forearms intrigue scientists. When considered alongside the grave goods found with his remains, scientists wonder if he might have been a drummer or some sort of shaman.

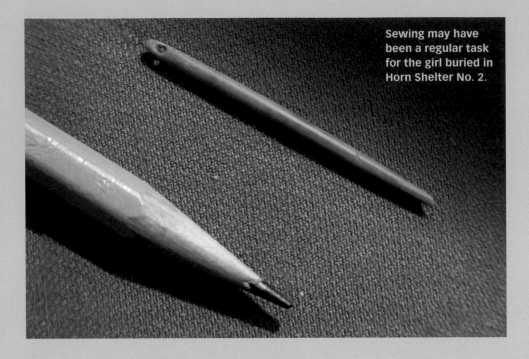

Sewing may have been a regular task for the girl buried in Horn Shelter No. 2.

apprentice. We have no way of knowing yet. What circumstances could have led to them being buried in a single grave? "It is tempting to think they were family members who died at the same time, perhaps of an infectious disease. However, this conclusion is a view in keeping with our culture today," Jodry said. "In fact, we don't know anything about the religious practices of their community. It is possible she was sacrificed and placed in the grave, perhaps as someone to help him in the next world, after death."

We do know something about the little girl. She could sew. A broken sewing needle made of bone lay in the area between her ribs and her left thigh, suggesting the needle may have been inside a pouch she wore tied around her waist. Had she stitched clothing or moccasins with this needle? Was it placed with her for use in an afterlife? A needle is a tool historically associated with women. The anthropologists considered this when they reassessed gender. But was that true in Paleoamerican cultures? We can only surmise.

We don't have to guess about one of the girl's habits. With the exception of one upper molar, all of the girl's teeth were permanent teeth. Her one remaining baby tooth was loose, and the permanent tooth beneath it was ready to slip into place. But first, that loose baby tooth had to come

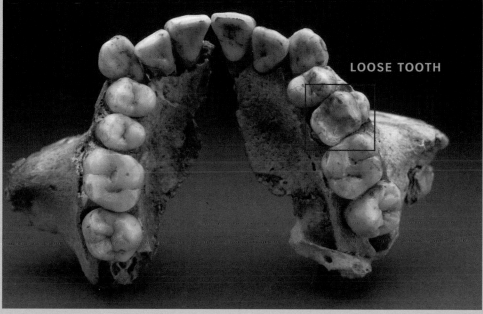

The only baby tooth left in the little girl's mouth was the second baby molar. Her food must have contained a lot of grit. Notice how worn the surface of the loose tooth is compared to the ridges on the other molars.

LOOSE TOOTH

out. Like any person with a loose tooth, the little girl would have been busy wiggling that tooth with her index finger and thumb or pushing it back and forth with her tongue. She died before the tooth came free.

Although their remains came to light more than four decades ago, the Paleoamericans from Horn Shelter continue teaching us more about their lives. Yet Kennewick Man could do nothing but remain silent as the 1996 calendar pages slowly turned into 1997 and then to 1998. Would he ever get his turn?

CHAPTER FIVE

KENNEWICK MAN'S TURN

ON APRIL 6, 1998, THE WHUP, WHUP, WHUPPING BEAT OF HELICOPTER ROTORS FLOODED THE AIR ABOVE KENNEWICK MAN'S GRAVESITE AS THE CHOPPER MANEUVERED ITSELF INTO POSITION. A huge bundle of rocks suspended on heavy cable hung from the whirring aircraft. And then it rained rocks. By April 14, a construction company hired by the Army Corps of Engineers had dropped nearly 1 million pounds (450,000 kg) of rocks and logs made of coconut fiber on top of the discovery site. Fast-growing willow and Russian olive trees were planted on top.

Where Spirit Cave and Horn Shelter remain protected and available for further study, the area surrounding Kennewick Man's discovery site is now inaccessible. Whether Kennewick Man had been buried near others became a question that could no longer be answered. Any grave goods he might have had are unlikely to emerge anytime soon. Now only his bones remained to tell his story, and their fate still rested in the courts.

A helicopter approaches the site where Kennewick Man's remains were discovered. Over the course of one week in 1998, helicopters like this one deposited 1 million pounds (450,000 kg) of rocks on the site as part of an erosion control measure ordered by the Army Corps of Engineers.

THE INVENTORIES

In October 1998, two years after Kennewick Man's remains were found, his journey in the United States court system had barely begun. Yet another journey was on his horizon. He was being moved from Battelle Laboratory to Seattle's Burke Museum, where a team of scientists hired by the federal government—none of whom were among the eight scientists suing to study Kennewick Man—planned to examine his skeleton. Several months earlier, addressing concerns about the safety of Kennewick Man's bones, Judge Jelderks had ordered a complete inventory of the bones be done before the move to Burke.

A report filed with the court back in the spring revealed that an anthropologist hired by the Justice Department to assess the skeleton's condition had reported four of the six pieces of Kennewick Man's femurs were missing. A recheck of Julie Longenecker's September 1996 inventory confirmed they weren't on her list either. Apparently, they had been missing for some time.

On the black market, ancient bones as famous as Kennewick Man's would be worth millions of dollars. The monetary value of his femurs paled in comparison to the information lost—the opportunity to confirm his height and weight the least of it. When had the pieces been taken? While they were in the sheriff's office? During their first five days at Battelle? Or some other time? Most importantly, where were they?

These questions were still unanswered when Judge Jelderks appointed Doug Owsley to conduct an inventory while he was assessing the overall condition of the skeleton. This authorized inventory would provide a detailed record of all the bones—one that could be consulted whenever Kennewick Man was examined. The Corps of Engineers allowed Owsley to choose only one person to assist him. He chose James Chatters, whose earlier examination of the bones placed him in a unique position of being able to assess the condition of the bones and whether they were deteriorating.

The inventory held on October 28 might be Owsley's only visit with Kennewick Man, and he was determined to make the most of his time. His marathon session began at quarter of seven in the morning. As tribal members looked on, three conservators (experts in the preservation and care of bones and artifacts) hired by the Corps of Engineers carried storage boxes containing Kennewick Man's remains into the laboratory. To avoid contaminating the bones with oils from his skin, Owsley pulled on a pair of latex gloves before handling them. Time didn't allow him to assemble multiple bone fragments. This made recognizing patterns of change on the entire bone extremely difficult—something crucial when an anthropologist is trying to determine how an individual may have received injuries or even chronically suffered from a disease.

Using a tape recorder, Owsley described each fragment of bone and its condition, noting features such as the shape of the skull or a fracture in a rib. He was forbidden to make any measurements of the bones.

Stopping only for a short dinner break, Owsley continued examining Kennewick Man. He noted the colors of the various bones. Chatters checked the width of the cracks in the cranium, finding that they had widened since he had last seen them, in August 1996. Midnight came and went. Yet the study continued. Finally, at two thirty in the morning, Owsley declared his inventory complete. His inventory noted that most of both femurs were missing. He helped the Corps of Engineers' representatives repack Kennewick Man's skeleton into the storage boxes. This time when Kennewick Man moved, there would be no uncertainty concerning which bones were present.

THE 1999 TEAM

Between 1998 and 2000, the United States Department of the Interior planned its own study of Kennewick Man's remains and assembled a team of scientists to do so (referred to as the 1999 team hereafter). The team included a number of anthropologists, geologists, experts in DNA analysis and radiocarbon dating, and a specialist in stone tools.

One of the questions the 1999 team hoped to answer was whether Kennewick Man could be conclusively connected with any of the modern tribes living in the area. The anthropologists compared Kennewick Man's skull and bones with modern Native Americans and with people from Asia, Polynesia, and Europe. The anthropologists' comparisons indicated that Kennewick Man more closely resembled people from Polynesia and southern Asia than Native Americans or Europeans. Unfortunately, the samples they removed in 2000 for DNA testing yielded inconclusive results. No definite conclusions about Kennewick Man and possible cultural affiliation could be drawn.

THE VERDICT

Finally, on August 2, 2002, almost eight years after the lawsuit was filed, after hearing, reading, debating, and reviewing a mountain of testimony, Judge Jelderks handed down his decision: the evidence had not led him to conclude Kennewick Man was affiliated with a modern tribe. Jelderks said he understood the position of the defendants (the U.S. government and the Department of the Army), particularly the geographic claim made by tribal members that their ancestors had occupied the territory for hundreds, perhaps thousands, of years. However, none of the submitted evidence convinced the judge that Kennewick Man hadn't been a traveler, one of many who moved along the river on a journey elsewhere. (Tribal claimants later filed an appeal to Jelderks's decision and its interpretation of NAGPRA, but the appeal was finally dismissed in 2004.)

Jelderks's ruling in favor of the eight scientists who were the plaintiffs in the lawsuit had one immediate effect. It gave the scientists forty-five days to submit a study plan to the Army Corps of Engineers. The plaintiffs wasted no time in developing it.

FBI

During the 1999 team's study, Kennewick Man's story added a new character and a new acronym—this time a famous one. The Federal Bureau of Investigation (FBI) stepped in to investigate the case of the missing femurs. The story briefly resembled a TV crime-scene investigation show again. Floyd Johnson took a lie detector test. James Chatters testified in court. Agents searched and questioned, but the pieces of femur were not found. So, in 2001, still at a loss to explain the disappearance, the FBI closed the case. And then, surprisingly, two months later, a box was found among materials that had been moved from Floyd Johnson's small evidence locker during a building renovation project. It was a box Johnson had never seen before. Inside it, in plastic bags, were the missing pieces of Kennewick Man's femurs. The whereabouts of the pieces for almost five years is unknown, but thankfully, for Kennewick Man's sake, they were recovered.

These are the two recovered pieces of Kennewick Man's left femur. If you mentally rotate the piece of bone in the top photo, you can see how its broken edge fits perfectly with the broken edge of the other piece (the knobby knee-end of the femur).

CONFIRM AND CONTINUE

As the scientists put together their plan, they had several specific goals designed to add new information to Kennewick Man's story. They included obtaining a sample of bone of more suitable quality for testing and sediment samples for further analysis; creating a final inventory of all the bones and teeth, including measurements; an extensive examination of the stone point embedded in the hip bone; and if possible, identifying where the skeleton came from and how it came to be in the water.

Independently verifying data is an important part of the scientific process. Accordingly, cross-checking the measurements and observations made by the 1999 study team was one of the 2004 team's first undertakings. They hoped to answer unresolved questions about his age, injuries, and the spearpoint. Another point of interest was determining how—if at all—his remains had been affected by the conditions surrounding the skeleton while it was in the ground, including damage by plants, animals, or erosion. Finally, they wanted to compare Kennewick Man with other Paleoamericans and with modern human populations from all over the world to see how they might be related.

Forensic anthropologists, a geologist, an archaeologist, an expert on paleopathology (how diseases affect bones and change their appearance), experts on the teeth of ancient people, and a photographer were among the members of the new study team. They scheduled new X-rays and CT scans made with the latest scanning equipment, yielding many more slices and much finer detail than earlier scans.

On three occasions between 2004 and 2006, the Corps of Engineers permitted various members of the 2004 team to work with Kennewick Man. Some findings corroborated earlier studies, while others contradicted them. All of them added more pieces to Kennewick Man's story.

REASSEMBLING THE SKELETON

After surveying the skeleton in 2004, the team tweaked their study plans and were ready for detailed work in July 2005. The team decided the best way for Kennewick Man to begin telling his story was by reassembling his skeleton, which was in 275 pieces (remember, the human skeleton has 206 bones). "We wanted to lay out the entire skeleton in anatomical order so we could evaluate patterns of breakage and bone discoloration. This is more easily seen when you can view all of the bones at once," explained skeletal biologist and forensic anthropologist Kari Bruwelheide. Usually forensic anthropologists lay the remains on a flat surface cushioned with a thin layer of a material called Ethafoam. However, this wouldn't work for Kennewick Man's fragmented bones. "A flat surface would not provide the support needed to keep the many separate pieces of bone in their proper places. We couldn't physically reattach the pieces—conditions set by the Corps of Engineers would not allow the use of glue, even that approved by conservators—so we had to devise a way to carefully and gently hold them together from underneath," Bruwelheide stated.

The team solved the problem by building a low wooden frame. "The frame was partially filled with sand, which acted as a soft support for the bones of the skeleton. We covered the sand with a black velvet cloth. I could then fit the bones together, propping them up with the sand, which cushioned and supported the bones from underneath without being seen."

Properly gloved, Bruwelheide focused on Kennewick Man. "When reassembling a skeleton I usually begin with the major elements, or larger bones. This allows me to gauge how much room is required for the entire skeleton. For example, if I start with the hipbones and femurs, I can work my way both up and down the skeleton knowing approximately how much space is needed to complete the layout," she explained. Bone by bone, she put each one into its correct place. Some bones, however, are harder to place than others. "The finger and toe bones, or phalanges, are definitely the hardest to sort from one another because they all look so similar. Only very slight differences allow you to sort them by left or right side and by digit," she added.

With Kennewick Man's bones in their proper places, the team revisited the issue of his age at the time of death. Determining the age of a person between middle and older age is a challenging task. In the 1940s, anthropologists thought Spirit Cave Man was a young adult. Later reexamination proved he was much older. Prehistoric remains further complicate the job because ancient lifestyles and activities were very different from those of modern people—the group whose skeletal features are usually used as age standards.

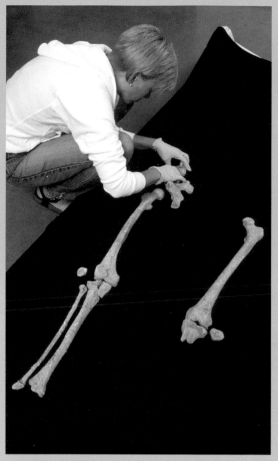

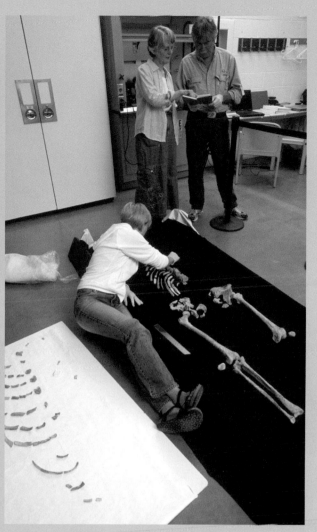

Piece by piece, Kari Bruwelheide assembled
Kennewick Man's skeleton. Physical
anthropologist Cleone Hawkinson and geologist
Tom Stafford are standing in the righthand photo.

Kennewick Man's signals regarding his age led the different teams
of researchers to different interpretations. Joseph Powell and Jerome
Rose, of the 1999 team, based their estimate of Kennewick Man's age on
his fused skull sutures, the bone surface on the back of his ilium, and
also on the bone surface at the front edge of his two hip bones, all of
which change with age. Based on their observations, Powell and Rose
concluded Kennewick Man was forty-five to fifty years old when he died.
In contrast, James Chatters initially estimated the age as between thirty-
five and forty-five. Because Kennewick Man's bones don't show a great
deal of the kinds of changes associated with advanced age—arthritis, for
example—and some of his bones still have some youthful features, the
2004 study team concluded he was approximately forty years old at the
time of his death.

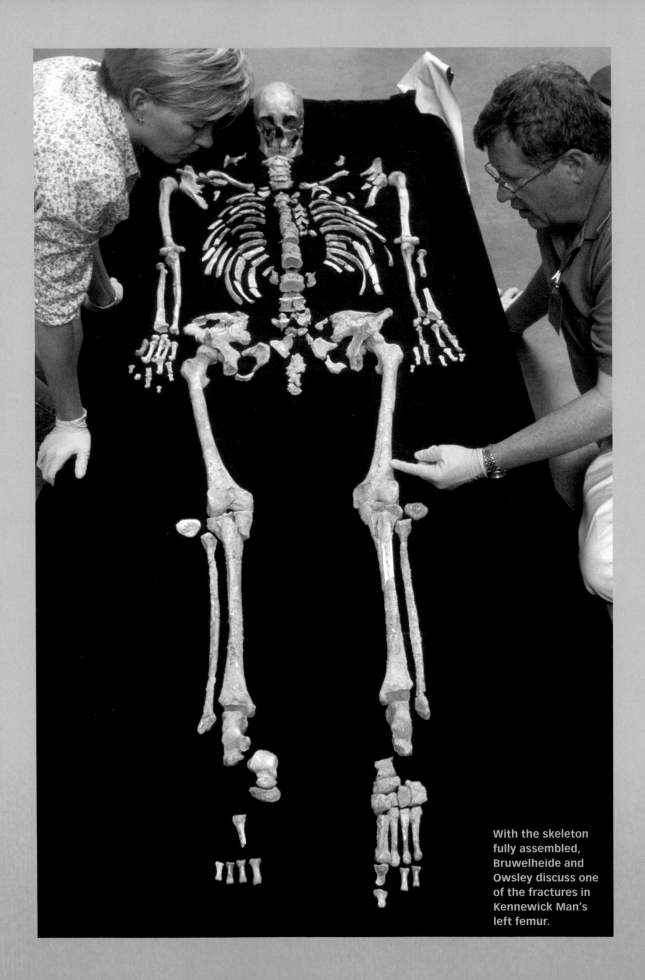

With the skeleton fully assembled, Bruwelheide and Owsley discuss one of the fractures in Kennewick Man's left femur.

The 1999 team estimated Kennewick Man's height using measurements made with calipers and calculations based on the length of his upper arm bones. (At that time, the femurs, bones ordinarily preferred for this estimate, were still missing.) This method yielded a height between 5 feet 9 inches and 5 feet 10 inches (1.8 m). Six years later, the 2004 team also measured Kennewick Man's bones—now including the recovered femurs—with calipers. The team created a database of measurements. This time, the height and length of the skull, the vertebrae, and the leg bones all became part of the calculations used to determine his height. These calculations, which take into account variations in muscle tissue, indicate that Kennewick Man was between 5 feet 6 inches and 5 feet 7 inches (1.7 m) tall. The difference in height estimates is the result of using new techniques to record and analyze information and because skeletal studies undertaken since the 1990s have taught scientists more about bones and how they relate to height. New studies yield new knowledge. A separate set of calculations, which included the estimate of Kennewick Man's height and the width of his pelvis, estimated his weight at about 160.9 pounds (73 kg). He was a sturdy, robust man.

With his skeleton reassembled and photographed, and his height and weight established, the team was eager to learn more. However, the Corps of Engineers' regulation

Team members share and compare their observations. They record the information they obtain by drawing diagrams, taking photographs, and entering data into computer programs.

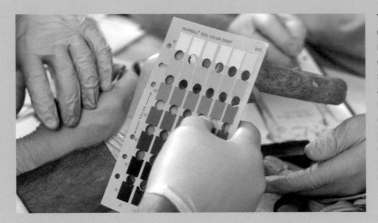

The Munsell Color Chart contains many color hues, each of which has a specific name. When a bone's color is identified with this chart, scientists not present at the time of examination can precisely know the color of every bone.

of the skeleton hampered some of their study plans. For example, the team was not allowed to remove any new samples of bone for isotope or radiocarbon dating analyses. They had to rely on fragments already taken from the skeleton by the earlier study team, even though the bones sampled were not necessarily the best ones suited for particular tests.

SKULL STORIES, SURFER'S EAR, AND TOOTH TALES

In July 1996, when Will Thomas reached into the water to play a joke on his friend Dave, he literally found himself face-to-face with Kennewick Man. Obviously, he knew he'd found a human skull—the spaces where the man's eyes and nose had been were unmistakable. But not being a trained anthropologist, Thomas was unable to recognize several features of the skull and teeth that offered some intriguing glimpses into Kennewick Man's life.

A small depression in Kennewick Man's forehead, about an inch and a half (4 cm) above his left eye, is the remaining proof of a clunk on the head that had enough force to dent his skull. As is the case with Spirit Cave Man's skull fracture (which was more severe), it's impossible to know the circumstances surrounding Kennewick Man's injury—if he fell forward and hit his head or if someone purposely hurt him. However, at least half of the male Paleoamerican skulls studied have similar head fractures. This type of injury is most often caused by violence. The impact of a rock thrown directly at Kennewick Man's head could cause this kind of skull fracture. Two things are certain about Kennewick Man's skull fracture: Unless he had been knocked unconscious, he probably clutched his head

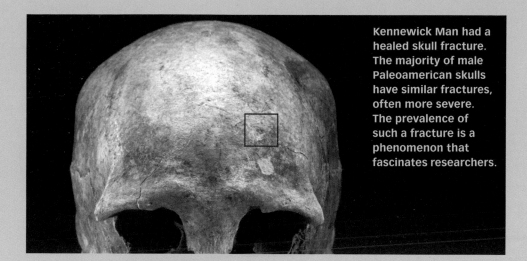

Kennewick Man had a healed skull fracture. The majority of male Paleoamerican skulls have similar fractures, often more severe. The prevalence of such a fracture is a phenomenon that fascinates researchers.

as most people reeling with a sudden head pain would. And secondly, the fractured bone was completely remodeled by the body's bone-repair processes, a sign the fracture had healed before Kennewick Man's death.

Although the fleshy part of Kennewick Man's ears decomposed long ago, the bony ear canal opening on each side of his skull where his ears had been is easy to see. A tantalizing clue about where Kennewick Man spent a lot of his time lies just inside each opening. During Kennewick Man's life, a raised, bony growth, called an auditory exostosis, developed on the bone surface along the bottom of his ear canals. Research suggests some exostoses are genetically passed from parent to child. But it also appears that environmental conditions can affect their growth. Many modern people who have auditory exostoses live, work, or play in or near water. In fact, the condition is often known as surfer's ear. People who spend a lot of time in wet, windy and, perhaps, seasonally cold conditions seem more likely than others to develop this growth. The bone growths inside Kennewick Man's ears suggest he spent a lot of time in wet, windy places. Perhaps other bone clues, when seen in combination with the exostoses, would suggest specific activities Kennewick Man might have done in a watery environment.

Kennewick Man's teeth added more chapters to his skull's stories. With the exception of two third molars—one lost sometime before he died and the other after death, most likely when his remains slid into the river—searchers at the discovery site had recovered all the rest of Kennewick Man's teeth, despite his mandible having broken into three pieces. Teeth are frequently dislodged from skeletal remains if the bones are jostled after death. That so many of Kennewick Man's teeth were present suggests a quick, permanent burial rather than a body left to decompose in the open, which would have led to bone scattering. Whether this quick, permanent burial was also intentional remained a question yet to be answered.

Christy G. Turner II is an expert on teeth. He has examined many thousands of teeth—modern and ancient—from various ancestries, including Asian, Arctic, European, North and South American, Australian, and African peoples. Dental traits, for example shoveling and the number of roots certain molars have, are passed from parents to their children. The 2004 study team hoped Turner could identify whether Kennewick Man's teeth offered clues about his ancestry, as well as his relationship, if any, to modern Indians.

Everyone who sees Kennewick Man's teeth quickly notices they are worn. Both James Chatters and the 1999 team reported that Kennewick Man's teeth showed characteristics associated with Southeast Asia, and also like the Ainu people of Japan, which differ from those typically found in ancient Northeast Asians and recent Native Americans. Turner disagreed with their conclusion for a couple of reasons. First, the crowns of most of his teeth—the enamel-covered part of a tooth seen above the gumline—were worn to the point where identifying key surface features, such as shoveling, wasn't possible. Secondly, Turner was unable to see the roots of molars still embedded in the jaws well enough to count and classify Kennewick Man's teeth. Turner concluded the information gleaned from Kennewick Man's teeth was insufficient for making any determinations about Kennewick Man's ancestry.

But Kennewick Man's teeth did offer the 2004 team some information. Had Kennewick Man been alive today, he would not have needed braces—his teeth were straight.

On the whole, Kennewick Man had healthy teeth, with no cavities. In comparison, later prehistoric hunter-gatherers who lived in the Northern California region did have cavities, due to differences in diet. For example, they ate a lot of acorns, which are high in carbohydrates, a sugary starch that if left on tooth surfaces tends to promote cavities.

Still, even without tooth decay issues, Kennewick Man was hard on his teeth. As he aged, abrasive material in his food slowly wore his teeth, as did some work-related tasks. The area where the crown meets the root had become the chewing surface of his teeth, a degree of wear rarely seen in modern people. Only the merest sliver of the enamel of his front teeth would have been visible when Kennewick Man smiled.

Why were his—and other Paleoamerican—teeth so worn? Chewing brings the upper and lower teeth into contact with each other. Over the years, this causes a slight degree of wear. Most foods a person eats are not hard enough to scratch and wear enamel. The real culprit for worn teeth is grit on, or in, the food. If food is not thoroughly washed, sediment particles can become part of the meal. Food-preparation methods can also introduce grit into the diet. For example, if Kennewick Man's people preserved meat and fish for the winter by drying them, they likely contained fine sediments blown onto their surface while they hung or lay in the sun. As anyone who has ever picnicked on a beach knows, if you eat near a beach, sand always finds its way into your food. The exostoses in his ear canals suggest Kennewick Man spent a lot of time near the water. He likely ate some meals there.

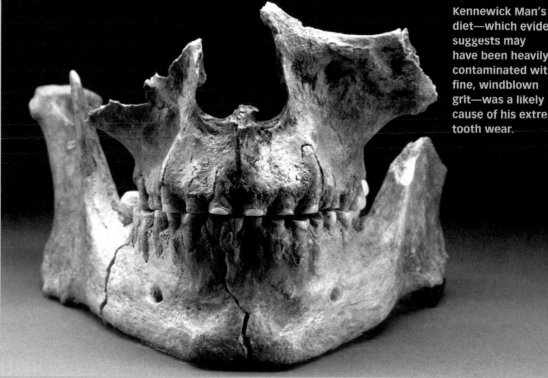

Kennewick Man's diet—which evidence suggests may have been heavily contaminated with fine, windblown grit—was a likely cause of his extreme tooth wear.

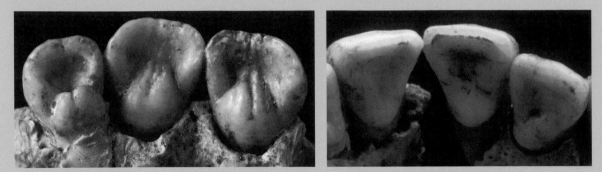

The trait called shoveling gives the incisors a scooplike appearance *(left)*. The incisors shown in the photo at the right are less shoveled. They belong to the girl from Horn Shelter *(see page 67)*. Kennewick Man's teeth were too worn to tell if they were shovel-shaped or not.

Mark Teaford, an expert on the wear patterns of teeth, examined Kennewick Man's teeth with a special microscope that highlights microwear patterns. Teaford saw fine scratches in keeping with sandy and silty soils found along rivers or on semiarid, grassy plains. Windblown grit on the surface of food would cause this kind of scratching. But the scratches weren't overly plentiful, suggesting Kennewick Man's food may have been washed to remove some of the sediment.

Looking at Kennewick Man's teeth does not tell us what he ate. But the carbon and nitrogen isotopes contained in his bones offer insight. Carbon isotopes reveal whether a diet consists of terrestrial or aquatic organisms. Kennewick Man's carbon isotopes told the 2004 study team that he ate mostly fish that were somehow connected to waters of the Pacific Ocean. For the Columbia River, this would be salmon (which live in the ocean but swim into the Columbia River to spawn), plus any fish, such as trout, that eat salmon (or their remains). When these fish eat salmon, their bodies absorb the carbon isotopes contained in the salmon's body.

"Nitrogen isotopes tell us how high Kennewick Man was on the food chain. These isotopes reveal whether he ate only plants or animals, such as deer or bison that only eat plants, or if he was high on the food chain eating animals that ate animals that ate plants," explained Tom Stafford. On land, top predators—foxes, bears, eagles, and humans—are high on the food chain. Seals are top predators in the ocean. "The nitrogen isotopes in Kennewick Man's bones indicated he was a high level predator," Stafford added. So, if Kennewick Man had lived near the place he was buried, he must have eaten a lot of salmon and fish, such as trout, and/or predators

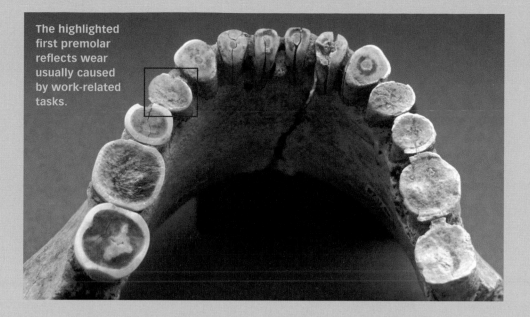

The highlighted first premolar reflects wear usually caused by work-related tasks.

that ate them. If he had lived on the coast, he would have eaten marine carnivores, such as seals. How long had Kennewick Man lived by the river? Or had he and his people only been passing through on a journey to or from the sea? Perhaps future researchers will definitively answer these questions.

Interestingly, certain worn areas on Kennewick Man's teeth do hint at his daily chores. When his jaws were closed, the biting surface of his upper- and lower-first premolars did not meet. That's because the lower tooth was worn, possibly by biting on some sort of cord to hold it in place during a task. Both Teaford and Turner noticed slight rounding on the front edges of three of his lower incisors and on the cheek side of his upper right first molar. This rounding is commonly found when people routinely use their teeth as a helping hand. (Think of holding a hard-to-open bag of chips in your teeth while using both hands to rip open the bag.) Perhaps Kennewick Man gripped a fishing cord with his teeth while his hands grabbed the fish. Maybe he worked on animal skins by holding part of the hide between his teeth. We don't know what Kennewick Man was doing, just that he relied on his teeth to help him complete his work.

Kennewick Man's astonishingly complete cranium and teeth are a huge help to researchers, to say nothing of how the skull quite literally gives this man a face. But as important as Kennewick Man's head is, it provides a relatively small part of the whole tale told by his skeleton. For those chapters, the rest of the skeleton is the storyteller.

CHAPTER SIX

A Body of Evidence

A PERSON'S HEAD MAKES THE CRITICAL DECISIONS—WHAT TO EAT, WHERE TO TAKE SHELTER, WHEN TO FIGHT, AND WHEN TO FLEE—BUT IT IS THE REST OF A HUMAN'S BODY THAT EXECUTES THEM. This was as true in Kennewick Man's time as it is now. Arms and legs, hands and feet all bear the marks of the decisions made in the head. And it was those marks that the team tried to read. Two questions uppermost in their minds were how would a man living in the Columbia River basin nine thousand years ago have spent his time? And how are those activities reflected in his bones?

LEGGING IT

In prehistoric times, survival was a full-time job. Kennewick Man had been busy gathering food. The muscle attachment sites on his bones should provide clues to his activities much the way the attachment sites found on the bones of Arch Lake Woman and Horn Shelter Man had.

Interestingly, the long bones of living athletes offer some insight about how ancient people may have used their arms and legs. Various scientific instruments can monitor the ways modern athletes use their arms and legs. Some of these instruments reveal the changes that occur in a long bone's shape as new material is added. Researchers have discovered that patterns of new bone growth sometimes differ according to the sport the athlete plays. For example, the repetitive motion of a cross-country runner's leg muscles leads to new bone on the runner's femurs and tibias (the larger of the two lower leg bones). Soccer players also develop strong leg bones. But playing soccer requires sharp, quick turns and sudden starts and stops. These motions require slightly different use of the muscles and stress leg bones in ways unlike the stresses of long-distance running, and so new bone is added to a soccer player's femurs and tibias in patterns and directions that reflect how the player used his or her muscles.

This digital rendering of Kennewick Man's right femur is based on a high-resolution CT scan commissioned by the 2004 team.

"Muscles place lots of stress on the bones by pulling on them. A bone's size and shape reflects the forces that are placed on it. The bone adapts by adding new material in certain directions to prevent the bone from excessive bending or twisting," explained Daniel Wescott, an anthropologist who specializes in how activity changes the long bones of human skeletons. "However, there is also a ground reaction force [when a leg makes contact with the ground] that places stress on the bones. As your foot hits the ground, your leg bones must absorb the forces from the impact."

Some bone changes caused by repetitive use and stressful forces are so great that even an untrained person can see the difference. Detecting others requires measurement, CT scans, and a specialist's eye. To discover what

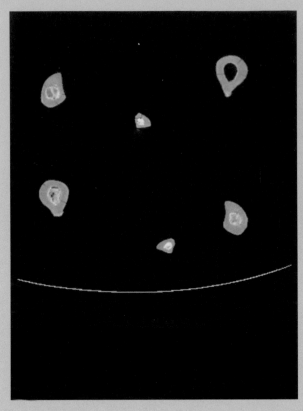

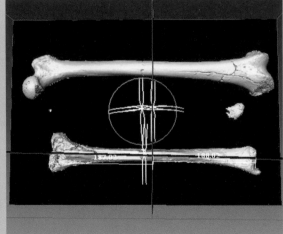

Left photo: Measuring the thickness of the bone walls in cross sections of Kennewick Man's long bones helped Wescott understand how the bone grew in response to repetitive use. *Top row, left to right:* Left tibia, fibula, and femur. *Bottom row, left to right:* Right femur, fibula, and tibia. *Photo above:* The top CT scan is the left femur. The scan clearly shows the fracture depicted in the photo on page 74. The lower CT scan is the left tibia.

kept Kennewick Man busy, Wescott examined data from high-resolution CT scans, made in 2006, of Kennewick Man's upper arm and leg bones. Since each slice was a specific cross section of a bone—a cross section is a view made by "cutting" straight across something—it showed the shape and diameter of the bone and its wall in that particular area. Additionally, a cross section slice shows what, if anything, is in the central part of the slice. Think of it as a way of seeing what's inside a bone without cutting it open.

When Wescott looked at the CT slices on his computer, he noticed each one had two main parts. Bone material of varying thickness rimmed the outer edge of each slice. The middle of each slice showed the bone's marrow chamber. Marrow is the soft, fatty substance that fills the hollow center of most bones. Kennewick Man's marrow had long since decomposed and disappeared, yet his marrow chamber was full. Sediment had filled the empty chamber in the years following Kennewick Man's death. Because the CT slices were so precise, Wescott quickly identified where bone material stopped and the sediment-filled marrow chamber started, making it easy to measure the bones' walls.

Kennewick Man had strong femurs, partially due to the size of his body. However, the cross section slices told Wescott that the bones were stronger and more robust than one might expect to find in another man of similar size and weight. Kennewick Man had used his thigh muscles a lot, in motions more like a soccer player's than a cross-country runner's. What kinds of activities can explain this?

Paleoamericans had to have a variety of skills if they wanted to live as long as Kennewick Man did. They hunted and fished with stone-tipped spears and darts. Nets woven of plant fibers caught fish and maybe small animals. Paleogatherers foraged for berries, seeds, and nuts. All of these activities place a variety of stresses on muscles, as does the land people trek across. The femurs of prehistoric European hunters of large prey—deer and elk, for example—were very strong, probably from following prey long distances over rugged terrain. In addition to strong femurs, the tibias of these hunters have noticeably raised muscle attachment sites. That's because climbing and descending place extra stress on the lower leg bones and the muscles that support them.

Kennewick Man had powerful legs. In fact, his femurs were stronger than those of other prehistoric hunters, especially those who had lived in Europe. Without doubt, Kennewick Man walked a lot. But the Columbia River basin—the area where Kennewick Man lived—was not rugged, mountainous terrain. "The landscape was not flat, though," explained James Chatters. "It had low sandy hills, with hummocks of grass. This surface is hard to walk on. To remain steady, your feet and ankles roll back and forth as you walk." Kennewick Man built strong leg muscles walking on terrain like this, and that would have affected his leg bones. The measurements Wescott made from the CT slices helped reveal how the bone in Kennewick Man's femurs had grown. The pattern was similar to that found in athletes who frequently change direction, again, like a soccer player. Remaining upright while walking up and down unstable, sandy hills would also have required Kennewick Man's leg muscles to shift constantly. What other activities might explain his strong legs?

Seeking more clues, Wescott turned to Kennewick Man's lower leg bones. They were strong. Obviously, he had relied on them. However, his tibias were not like those of the prehistoric long-distance European hunters. Unlike them, the size and shape of Kennewick Man's tibias told Wescott that Kennewick Man had spent a lot of time not only changing

These porous areas of bone on the femur and tibia, at the back of the knee, occur when a knee is tightly flexed for long periods of time. Rather than sitting cross-legged on the ground, Kennewick Man knelt—knees on the ground—with his rear end settled on his heels.

direction as he moved but that he had done so rapidly while he was running. In other words, sudden bursts of speed interspersed with equally sudden stops and turns.

One activity that can explain the kind of leg strength and development Kennewick Man had is small-game hunting. As he zigzagged in pursuit of small prey like rabbits, hopping around rocks and scooting in and out of shrubbery, Kennewick Man relied on strong legs for more than just running. He needed legs strong enough to power sudden bursts of speed, robust enough to withstand the impacts of sudden stops, and flexible enough to accommodate abrupt twists without injury. (Perhaps Kennewick Man could have dodged Sydney Wheeler's rattlesnake without hobbling for days afterward.)

Yet another activity can create the kind of bone development shown by Kennewick Man's legs. Nine thousand years ago, the Columbia basin region was not as dry as it is today. Instead, rivers and streams—plentiful with fish—flowed across the land. The carbon and nitrogen isotope levels in Kennewick Man's bones suggested he ate a lot of fish, so it seems certain he spent a lot of time spearfishing (fish hooks were not used in the region at that time), maybe even netfishing. Both types of fishing require the fisher to trudge in the water. A fisher who wades against river currents develops strong thigh muscles. At the same time, the effect of water supporting his weight would have reduced the stress on his lower leg bones. So traveling through water could explain why Kennewick Man's tibias were strong, yet did not show the kind of bone growth found in a person who had climbed steep terrain. (And being a regular fisher, constantly near water, could also explain the auditory exostoses found in Kennewick Man's ears.)

Interestingly, more than strong legs, surfer's ear, and carbon and nitrogen isotopes tie Kennewick Man closely to the Columbia River. Oxygen isotopes in his bones do too. Our bones readily absorb oxygen isotopes that come from the water we drink. Kennewick Man's oxygen isotopes suggest that he drank water from the Columbia River. Nine thousand years ago, most of the river's water came from melting mountain glaciers farther upstream. How did the 2004 team know that his drinking water was from the river and not rainwater? The oxygen isotopes of glacier water are different from rainwater that falls in Kennewick, Washington, or along the Pacific coast. While the oxygen isotopes in a person's bones can change, it takes a long time—probably more than ten to fifteen years. Kennewick Man's oxygen isotopes suggest he lived most of his life in the region where he was buried, but he may have been born elsewhere. Isotope analysis using the enamel from one of his teeth would conclusively determine his geographic origin—whether it was near Kennewick or from somewhere else.

Kennewick Man's leg bones tell us he was a very active person who from a very young age relied heavily on his legs. Logically, he used various hunting strategies—running, trudging, and shifting direction—as necessary to capture prey.

In 1996, when James Chatters first examined Kennewick Man's remains, he noticed that Kennewick Man's left leg, especially his thigh bone, appeared stronger than the right leg. Wescott's studies confirmed this: even though Kennewick Man had two strong legs, the left one was stronger. People usually use one hand more than the other, depending on right- or left-handedness. Had Kennewick Man used his left leg more heavily than his right? And if so, why?

A Bone of Contention

Certain scientific tests, radiocarbon dating for example, require the destruction of bone. Maximum bone preservation is always desired, so scientists try to minimize the amount of bone they must remove for laboratory testing. Kennewick Man's left tibia was the only complete long bone from his legs.

The 1999 study team removed a large section of that tibia for laboratory analyses such as radiocarbon dating, isotope analysis, and to obtain DNA (which ultimately proved unrecoverable). Testing at that time required larger samples of bone material. According to Tom Stafford, more recent techniques for the same studies are much more precise and accurate, so they only need a small sample. (The 1999 bone samples were fifty times larger than those necessary today.)

Because of their large diameter and thicker walls, the humerus, femur, and tibia are the first choice for laboratory analyses. These bones also contain important features that scientists use to determine how the bone was used. When large portions are removed, evidence of bone use can be lost. So the least amount of damage done to any of these bones, the better.

All Stafford's recent laboratory analyses of Kennewick Man's bones were made using the few grams remaining of the piece of tibia sample removed by the 1999 study team. Still, using only those bits, Stafford was able to obtain enormous amounts of data.

The 1999 study team removed a very large section of the left tibia for laboratory tests.

SPEARED!

Today when a person is sick or injured, doctors combat infection with antibiotics and antiseptics. Surgeons repair fractured bones. Physical therapists help restore mobility to damaged joints. In Paleoamerica, a person suffering with infection often died. Broken bones healed without casts or surgery as best they could—if they healed at all. Early researchers who examined Kennewick Man's skeleton suggested he'd suffered multiple fractures, many of them to his ribs. Kennewick Man was no stranger to pain, everyone agreed. However, the 2004 team disagreed with the earlier assessments of at least some of the rib injuries. Kennewick Man's ribs were broken into eighty pieces. Most of these breaks occurred when the bones fell from the riverbank. That said, Kennewick Man had fractured some of his ribs during his life. One of his left ribs had broken and healed before death. The anthropologists saw clear evidence of bone remodeling.

The appearance of at least five of his right ribs—each rib broken in only one place—was more perplexing. The broken edges looked as though they'd been "pinched" together. Had the ribs broken after death? It's difficult to imagine a force capable of exerting the multiple pressures needed to create a series of separate pinches. The likely explanation for this pinched appearance is that Kennewick Man fractured these ribs earlier in his life. Motionless, relaxing recovery time was not an option for Paleoamericans, not when survival was at stake. Movement during the daily activities required for survival continually shifted the broken edges of his right ribs and prevented them from knitting together. But more evaluation and study are necessary to fully understand and resolve these fractures and their significance.

At some time after he reached adulthood, Kennewick Man fractured his right shoulder. The break was caused when the ball-shaped end of his right humerus jammed upward and flaked off a piece of the shoulder bone. The loose piece of bone "floated" around in his shoulder afterward. This kind of break is rare, but it has happened in the baseball world, when a pitcher suddenly whips his throwing arm back to fire off a 90-mile-an-hour (145 km) fastball. For a pitcher, it's a career-ending injury. This injury, like the ones to Kennewick Man's left rib and his skull, healed before death, but it would have caused him discomfort and likely affected his ability to throw a spear.

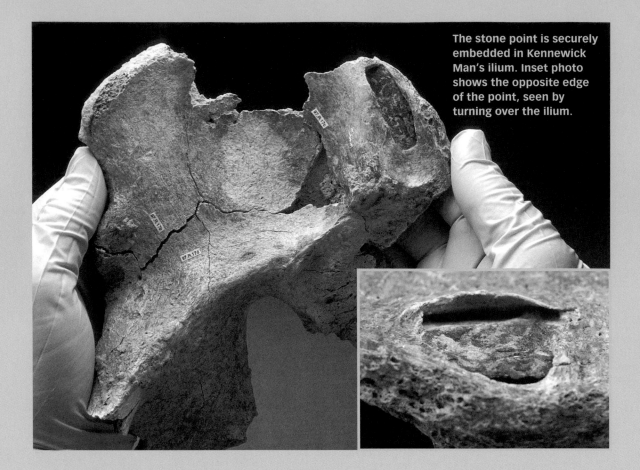

The stone point is securely embedded in Kennewick Man's ilium. Inset photo shows the opposite edge of the point, seen by turning over the ilium.

Kennewick Man's most severe injury by far was the one to his hip. When the spear smashed into his right ilium, there can be no doubt that the pain was agonizing, perhaps lasting for months. But the scientists who have studied the injury disagree on how it affected his movement afterward, underscoring the importance of reexamination and discussion.

In 1996, after studying the first CT scans of Kennewick Man's ilium, James Chatters felt sure Kennewick Man had seen the spear flying at him. The point's angle of entry and its orientation and position in Kennewick Man's right ilium suggested he could have. If he had, twisting his body toward the left trying to avoid being hit would make sense and might explain why the point entered his body where it did. Next, Chatters showed the scans to an orthopedic surgeon. The two men concluded Kennewick Man suffered from osteomyelitis, a form of chronic bone infection, at the site of the injury. Their belief was based on their interpretation of how the bone was remodeled during the healing process. A lot of new bone had been added, so they were sure Kennewick Man lived many years after he received the injury.

Knowing Kennewick Man had strongly developed legs, Chatters felt certain that the injury had been inflicted after Kennewick Man reached adulthood. Bones develop a good deal of their strength during the teen and young adult years, and he believed Kennewick Man's femurs and tibias reflected this. If, as a teen or a young man, he'd been unable to walk properly for a long period of time, his bones would not have developed as normally as they had. However, without strong antibiotics, Chatters and the doctor he consulted didn't think it seemed likely that a wound this severe could heal completely. As a result, they concluded the wound was chronically infected, meaning pus may have occasionally drained out of his body near the wound site. Both felt Kennewick Man would have been in pain when he walked. Had he limped, coming down heavy on his left leg as he avoided placing weight on his painful right hip and leg? Might limping account for having a stronger left leg?

The 1999 team made new CT scans of the ilium. Joseph Powell and Jerome Rose reviewed the scans and saw things differently from Chatters. They concluded the bone surrounding the stone point had completely healed long before Kennewick Man died. Further, they felt if infection had been associated with the wound, it had been minor and had left no evidence. They believed the spearpoint had entered the hip from the rear, with Kennewick Man's back toward his attacker, and that no major organs, blood vessels, or muscles had been damaged. Both believed Kennewick Man would have healed rapidly. Finally, they concluded Kennewick Man had suffered the injury when he was between fifteen and twenty years old.

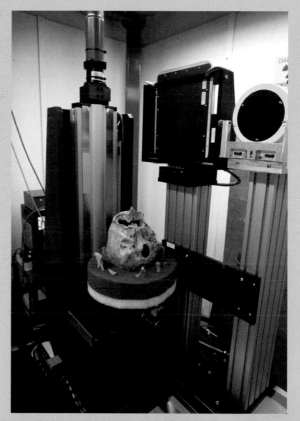

The CT scans commissioned by the 2004 study team used a level of radiation unsafe for scanning a living person. The increased radiation permitted finer, more detailed slices.

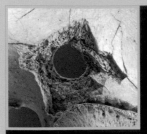

The bullet cleanly entered this man's ilium. However, it tore large fragments from the other side of the bone *(inset)* as it exited and passed into his abdomen. The man died within moments.

The 2004 team reexamined the ilium with new X-rays and with a new, stronger CT scanner capable of making extremely fine slices. From their CT scans, they also created a cast of the ilium and of the stone point. (All casts of the spearpoint are derived from the CT scan. Removing the point from the ilium would damage the bone.) By doing so, they hoped to determine definitively the trajectory of the spear and how it entered Kennewick Man's body. To further study the healing process, team members Doug Owsley and Kari Bruwelheide decided to compare Kennewick Man's injury with other pelvic injuries caused by a weapon, although these wounds were caused by bullets rather than spearpoints.

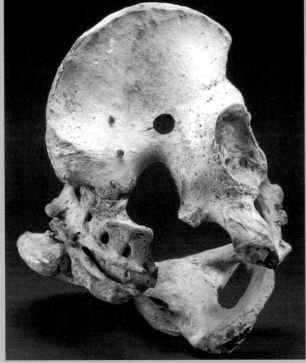

Infection festered in this soldier's ilium for a period of months and eventually led to his death.

The bone healed around the bullet wound in this ilium. The soldier lived many years afterward.

As the wound healed, the bone repaired itself by adding material that walled off the intrusive point.

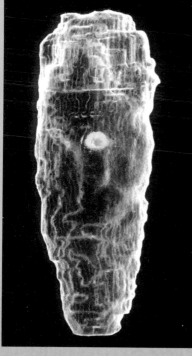

The high resolution CT scans gave the 2004 team all the information needed to make a cast of the stone point. The cast is made of a clear synthetic material.

The National Museum of Health and Medicine in Washington, D.C., has a collection of pelvic bones from soldiers and civilians wounded during wars in the nineteenth century. Bruwelheide and Owsley examined bones in the collection that showed three stages of gunshot injuries. Some wounds led to immediate death. The second group included wounds that festered with infection leading to the soldier's death. The last group contained wounds that had completely healed and the soldier died of an unrelated cause. By comparing Kennewick Man's hip with those of wounded civilians and soldiers, the two anthropologists clearly saw how an injured pelvic bone responds over time to wounds and infection, including walling off an embedded object from the rest of the bone by adding new material. They concluded sufficient time had passed for the bone to grow around the base of the spearpoint and that Kennewick Man's injury had healed by the time of his death. So all the investigators agreed Kennewick Man had most likely been a young adult and not a child when he received the wound. The exact circumstances of how he received the injury are a mystery. Perhaps it was combat between two bands of people. There is little doubt that someone intended to kill him. Had the point entered at a different angle, it would have entered Kennewick Man's bowels and he would have died.

Based on the point's angle of entry, the 2004 team agreed with Chatters that Kennewick Man had twisted his body attempting to dodge the spear. Had he seen his attacker approach, or was he ambushed? No one knows. When the spear slammed into Kennewick Man's body and the stone point struck his ilium, it sheared nearly an inch (2.5 cm) from the top of the bone. The tip of the point shattered on impact, and the spear's force would have knocked him down. The pain was intense. Despite the pain, either he or someone with him pulled the shaft of the spear away from the base of the point. The point itself was wedged too tightly into the bone to remove it. And then they stanched the bleeding.

During the days immediately following the injury, Kennewick Man could barely stand. Shock and pain left him weak. He needed care and help. Without the aid of others, he would have died. Those he lived with cleaned his wound. They brought him food and water. Slowly, his people nursed him back to health.

That Kennewick Man recovered from this injury tells us about the community he lived in. His people were hunter-gatherers (agriculture was not practiced in the area at that time), so caring for him would have taken time otherwise spent finding food. Yet they cared enough to do so, perhaps because Kennewick Man's skill as a hunter was necessary for their survival too.

During his recovery period, Kennewick Man almost certainly limped, at least temporarily. But he wasn't a person who gave up easily. He was a survivor. As time passed, his wound healed. And in the long run, the 2004 team didn't think the injury affected his gait or the overall strength of his legs.

So recalling Wescott's questions about the strength of Kennewick Man's left leg, if a limp doesn't explain why his left leg was more robust, what else would? Ironically, considering a spear caused his injury, Kennewick Man's right arm and the way he would have thrown a spear has provided an answer.

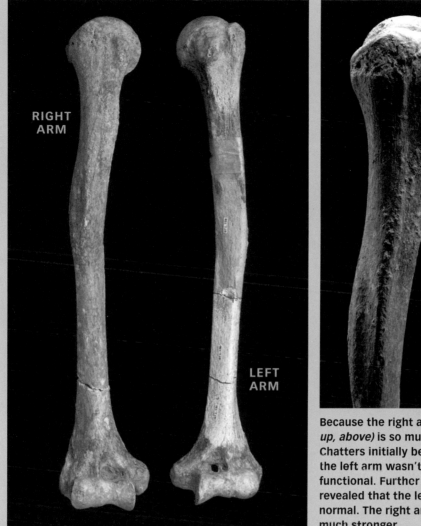

RIGHT
ARM

LEFT
ARM

Because the right arm *(close up, above)* is so much stronger, Chatters initially believed that the left arm wasn't entirely functional. Further study revealed that the left arm is normal. The right arm was just much stronger.

A RIGHT-HANDED GUY

A spear hunter's spear must not only reach his or her prey, it must do so with enough power to either instantly kill the prey or injure it so it can't escape. Kennewick Man wanted his throw to have distance and power, and he generated both with his well-developed right arm. Direct measurements made with calipers and those Wescott obtained from CT scan cross sections show that Kennewick Man's right arm was stronger than his left. The muscle attachment sites on his right humerus were very well-developed, as were the attachment sites for his shoulder and chest muscles. All the scientists who have come to know him agreed he was right-handed, and all agree when Kennewick Man hunted with a spear, it definitely affected his muscles.

Kennewick Man used an atlatl to increase the power of his throw. The person in this photo is gripping the atlatl's handle. His fingertips hold a tool called a foreshaft. A spearpoint is attached to the foreshaft. The other end of the foreshaft is wedged into a longer spear shaft during a hunt. Using a foreshaft makes it easier to remove an embedded spear from downed prey.

Kennewick Man also would have relied on a tool called an atlatl (AT-lattle) to generate distance and power. An atlatl is about the length of your forearm and is notched on one end. Atlatls are made of wood, bone, or ivory. An atlatl acts as a lever, adding speed and power to a throw, the same way a ball-pitching machine does. It propels a spear or dart many yards farther than an unaided throw. To throw his spear, Kennewick Man first wedged the end of the spear into the atlatl's notched end. Holding the other end, he flung the spear using his upper arm muscles. During the forward motion of the throw, he twisted and extended the muscles of his shoulder and upper arm as he rotated his arm to carry the spear forward. James Chatters described the motion as similar to that of a baseball pitcher or of a javelin thrower. And then Kennewick Man used his left leg. Surprisingly, throwing right-handed affects the left leg.

When Kennewick Man committed to a target, he moved toward his prey, seeking to be as close as possible and in the best place for an accurate throw. If he was a good hunter, he wasn't tentative when he struck. He put all of his energy into bringing down the animal he hunted. When he actually threw the spear, he would have stopped suddenly with almost all of his weight bearing down on his left leg, positioning it slightly ahead of his body, to make the stop. Simultaneously, he pulled back his right arm and rocked back onto his right leg. Then he shifted his weight back onto his left leg, which was firmly planted to absorb the force of the throw. "A right-handed bowler does the same thing, by planting his or her left leg just before throwing the ball. This causes significant force between the leg and the ground. The stress that this places on the left leg causes more bony material to be added to the lower leg bones to prevent damage," said Wescott. Like a right-handed pitcher or bowler, Kennewick Man's stronger left leg is totally consistent with what would be expected for a right-handed person who regularly hunted with a spear.

Rather than evidence of a disability, Kennewick Man's leg asymmetry suggests to scientists that he was physically very strong and athletic.

GET A GRIP

After a body decomposes, small bones, such as those of the hands and feet, are easily transported away from the rest of a skeleton. For this reason, the hands and feet of Paleoamericans are seldom found intact. In 1996 Chatters and others spent days collecting Kennewick Man's remains from the riverbed. Their careful scrutiny of the mud was time well spent: They found thirty-two of Kennewick Man's fifty-four hand bones. They also found twenty-five of Kennewick Man's fifty-two foot bones. Fortunately, the hand and foot bones that were recovered were well-preserved, adding to the knowledge of Paleoamerican hands and feet.

The backs of these hand bones are free from concretion.

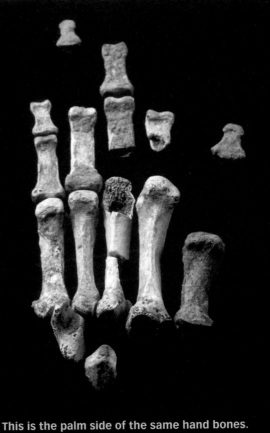

This is the palm side of the same hand bones. Notice that there is concretion on many of these bones. This later helped the 2004 study team determine the hands' position in the grave.

Reassembling a mix of these bones into their correct positions is a difficult task, one that fell to D. Troy Case, an anthropologist who specializes in the hand and foot bones of prehistoric human skeletons. The differences between the bones of the right and left hands may be very small. To further complicate the matter, some hand and foot bones closely resemble one another. Case made some changes to the 1999 team's grouping of these bones. He reassigned some hand and foot bones from one side to the other. He also moved two bones, which had been misidentified as foot bones, to the hands. Next, he measured the hand bones and visually examined the muscle attachment sites, seeking insight into how Kennewick Man habitually used his hands.

Humans grip objects with their hands in two ways. One is a power grip, where the fingers encircle an object, pressing it firmly against the palm. Kennewick Man held a club with a power grip. In contrast, Horn

Shelter Girl sewed using a precision grip, holding her needle between her thumb and one or two fingers. When Kennewick Man crafted stone tools, he used both grips. Since he was right-handed, he held a stone core tightly in his left hand with a power grip. In his right hand, he held a tool called a hammerstone with his thumb and several fingers. Using the precision grip, he struck flakes from the core, shaping the tool until it had a sharp edge. The two grips place different stresses on specific hand bones and muscles. By comparing the bones of the right hand with those of the left, Case is certain Kennewick Man most often used his right hand when the activity called for a precision grip.

A researcher would expect to learn these things from hand bones, but a good researcher would also be open to surprises as she or he examined the bones of each individual. In a most unexpected way, Kennewick Man's hands and feet helped answer an important question a lot of people had asked: *had people he knew intentionally buried his body, or had natural forces simply covered it?*

CHAPTER SEVEN

GRaVe MaTTeRS

**EVER SINCE THOMAS AND DEACY FIRST
PULLED KENNEWICK MAN'S SKULL FROM
THE RIVER, THE QUESTION "HOW DID HE
GET THERE?"** has been an intriguing one. If
Kennewick Man had died accidentally, away from
his people, his body might have been buried only
as a consequence of the accident. For example, if
he had drowned, his body might have been swept
downriver and lost. In contrast, the bodies of Arch
Lake Woman, the Horn Shelter No. 2 people, and
Spirit Cave Man were deliberately placed in their
graves in certain positions. Accidental burials
rarely result in a grave with the deceased's body
carefully positioned as these people's bodies were.
So the position of a body tells a lot about the
circumstances of a person's burial.

Kennewick Man's remains were scattered
along the shore of the Columbia River. It seemed
as though determining his position at the time of
burial would not be possible. Because the skeleton

was so complete, the 1999 team thought his burial was intentional, but they couldn't prove it. When the 2004 team looked more closely at Kennewick Man's bones, they knew understanding the circumstances of Kennewick Man's burial would require them to reconstruct the entire sequence of events that led to his skeleton landing in the river. And as usual, they'd have to do so without an obvious beginning, middle, or end.

HARD EVIDENCE

It's hard to imagine proving Kennewick Man had been buried in an intentional grave, much less reconstructing his body's position in that grave. Such a feat would seem unlikely even in a crime-scene investigation TV show. After all, nearly a decade had passed since Kennewick Man's scattered bones were found, and the discovery site is now buried under tons of rock. Yes, it's hard to imagine, but the scientists did it anyway.

The calcium carbonate concretions on the skeleton—the same ones that had caught Chatters's eye almost ten years earlier—provided compelling evidence of an intentional burial. In 1997 the Corps of Engineers approved the removal of a limited number of sediment samples from the riverbank near the discovery site. By analyzing the sediment layers in the samples and comparing them with sediments adhering to Kennewick Man's bones, investigators hoped they could determine when and where his remains had been buried.

When geologist Thomas Stafford and other investigators were sampling the sediment, they saw small, knobby nodules of concretions scattered in the mud. And when Chatters had examined Kennewick Man's bones in his laboratory, he'd seen a crusty coat of concretion on a number of them—it had even obscured his view of the spearpoint. Stafford was intrigued by a layer in the riverbank that contained concretions.

Stafford is familiar with these kinds of nodules and the way they form. According to Stafford, the process started with rain. "Rainwater passing through the atmosphere picks up carbon dioxide. This forms a solution of a weak acid called carbonic acid that dissolves some types of rock and any calcium carbonate already existing in the area. The solution percolates, or trickles downward, through the sediment." But at some point—the exact depth varies according to the soil and the region—

the solution dries up. As it does, the calcium carbonate precipitates, or forms a solid substance, as part of the drying process. This solid calcium carbonate sticks to grains of sediment. Over time, additional calcium carbonate accumulates around the grains, eventually forming the knobby concretions found at the Kennewick discovery site. The calcium concretions formed about two thousand years ago.

When the calcium-rich solution encounters larger materials—like rocks—it flows around them, and instead of forming nodules, it forms a crust on the underside of the rocks. "The sediment where Kennewick Man was buried was almost entirely fine sands and coarse silt," Stafford continued. "In this instance, the calcium-rich solution treated Kennewick Man's skeleton as if it had been a group of large rocks. The solution trickled around his bones and precipitated on whatever part was facing downward," Stafford explained. The calcium concretion Chatters and others noticed on Kennewick Man's bones was clearly connected to this layer of sediment. Amazingly, his skeleton had lain where the calcium concretion layer had formed.

2 mm

The crusty concretion on the underside of this rock and the concretion on Kennewick Man's bones formed by the same process.

Calcium concretion fused these two foot bones together. The bones are beside each other as they would have been when Kennewick Man was alive.

The pattern of concretion on Kennewick Man's bones indicated he lay horizontally in his grave, with his legs fully extended. However, the crust gradually increased on his lower leg bones and feet, in some places completely encircling the bone. These bones were several inches deeper within the calcium carbonate layer than those of Kennewick Man's upper body. The bottom of his grave had likely been slightly slanted, and his feet lay at the deeper end of the grave.

His arms had been placed along his sides. The concretion on his hand bones was solely on the palms' surface, telling us that his hands laid palm downward. If his hands had been positioned across his pelvis—as many European settlers hands were placed—concretions would have been evident at the points where the hands touched the pelvic bones. There was no corresponding concretion in those areas. Furthermore, concretion "glued" some of Kennewick Man's bones together. This proved those bones were next to one another in the grave. And because these bones were in the positions they occupied while he was alive, they further prove Kennewick Man's bones were articulated, or still together, when he was placed in his grave. As Thomas Stafford concluded, "He was not a jumble of bones and he was not a drowning victim who would have come to rest face-down." The new look at Kennewick Man found hard evidence that proved Kennewick Man was intentionally buried by people who carefully placed his body in the grave.

Red Stains, Red Herring

Some features of the skeleton that initially appeared to be evidence of intentional burial did not hold up to scrutiny. In 1999 Powell and Rose noticed red stains on one of Kennewick Man's hand bones, some ribs, and a lower leg bone. They speculated the stains may have been red ocher—possible evidence of intentional burial. Ocher is a pigment made of minerals that contain iron. When iron chemically reacts with oxygen and water, it turns various shades of yellow and red. For tens of thousands of years, humans have ground ocher, sometimes mixing it with sand or clay for use in ceremonies—like funerals— and as medicine. As a result, ocher is often found in graves. Ocher staining was found in Arch Lake Woman's grave, and a lump of ocher was in the Horn Shelter grave among the tools.

However, upon further examination, Phillip Walker, another scientist on the 1999 team, determined the stains had been caused after burial, probably by natural processes. Plant roots often intrude into graves. Chemical reactions occur when decomposing roots come in contact with skeletal remains, frequently causing red stains, particularly if iron is present. The 2004 team reinspected each bone for discoloration and staining. They confirmed the staining to be from natural processes and saw no verifiable red stains that could be attributed to cultural burial practices.

ARCH LAKE

HORN SHELTER

A THEORY TO CHEW ON

There was literally no mark on Kennewick Man's remains too small for the study teams to examine. In fact, some small marks on several bones revealed secrets out of proportion with their size.

Rodents dig into graves, and so it is not uncommon for archaeologists to find tooth marks on the bones. When a rodent gnaws, it leaves a pattern of distinctive grooves. In 1999 Powell and Rose interpreted marks on Kennewick Man's right arm and hand, his fibulas, and a rib as the tooth marks made by small- to medium-sized animals. They further noted gnaw marks on his right ulna describing them as light in color, showing no staining from soil lying against them. This, they speculated, was because rodents had gnawed the bone when it lay exposed on the beach shortly before the skeleton was discovered.

The 2004 team reexamined the marks and concluded they do not exhibit the characteristic grooves made by rodent teeth. Instead, the team believes the marks are more consistent with dings and nicks caused by waterborne sticks that hit the bones while they were partially exposed in the bank and after they fell from the bank and lay on the river bottom. At these times, sediment no longer protected them.

The 1999 study team attributed these nicks to rodent gnawing. The 2004 study team came to a different conclusion.

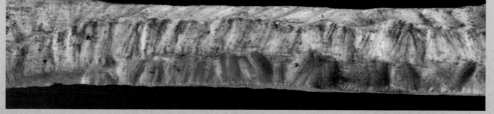

When rodents gnaw a bone, their teeth scrape pieces off in a pattern like the marks on the lower bone.

These marks were leading to the development of a theory about Kennewick Man's position in the riverbank, before it landed in the water—one that not only explained the gouges, but also explained a series of abrasions found on some bones on his left side. Kennewick Man himself supplied the explanation of how he left the riverbank, but only after he gave the team the information they needed to "return" him to it—not physically but through critical thinking.

OUT OF THE BANK AND INTO THE RIVER

Rising and falling water levels, wind, waves, and river current continually sculpt the Columbia's banks. Dramatic changes are not unusual. In less than a year, the riverbank at Kennewick Man's discovery site had eroded 6 feet (1.8 m) farther back from its position in July of 1996.

The effects of erosion also broke many of Kennewick Man's bones. In fact, most of his fractures occurred after death, when his skeleton dropped from the bank. These postmortem fractures, which happened at many different times, had the potential to provide convincing evidence of not only his burial position but how his bones eroded from the riverbank. To determine how this happened, forensic anthropologist Hugh Berryman's first task was identifying which breaks occurred while Kennewick Man's skeleton lay in his grave and which ones occurred when his bones fell to the shore.

The color of the fractured bone surfaces provided one clue. Over time, bone surfaces become stained by material in the soil. When a bone breaks at the time of death or shortly after burial, all of its surfaces—even fractured surfaces—become similarly discolored. When a bone breaks years after burial, the outer surface of the bone is already stained, but the newly exposed fractured surface is not. "Fractured surfaces with little staining probably occurred around the time the riverbank collapsed releasing the bones into the river," said Berryman. While color was a helpful clue, he knew it couldn't be the only consideration.

Berryman further examined the fractures. Human bones contain minerals and collagen. Minerals give bone the strength and rigidity to withstand compressive, or squeezing, forces. Collagen is elastic and allows bones to withstand tensile, or pulling, forces. Thus, a bone under mild pressure will bend slightly, without fracturing, and return to its original shape after the pressure is removed. As years passed, Kennewick Man's bones dried and lost elasticity as their collagen level decreased. Dry, brittle bone fractures more easily than fresh bone. "The pressure of heavy soil and rock, along with the effects of wet and dry periods—which causes bones to expand and shrink—cracked some of the brittle bones. These fractures open up parallel to the length of the bones, rather than breaking the bones in half, like a cross section," explained Berryman. For the pressure of the sediment to cause these parallel fractures to form, Kennewick Man must have been lying on his back. This

After minutely examining fracture surfaces, Berryman drew his observations on diagrams of the bones.

observation supported the 2004 team's theory about Kennewick Man's position in his grave.

Berryman also detected a number of smaller fractures, most of which were on the skeleton's left side. They suggest his left side may have been exposed for a longer period of time than his right. With Kennewick Man lying on his back, the simplest explanation for how his left side came to be exposed first is that his left side faced the river, where it was closer to wave action. For this to be so, the skeleton lay oriented with Kennewick Man's head upstream from his feet.

By combining information from the different kinds of postmortem bone fractures with the pattern of concretion found on many of the bones, the 2004 study team accomplished a task many believed impossible—they figuratively restored Kennewick Man's skeleton back into the riverbank.

Successive Stages of Long Bone Fracture

Figure 1. Sediment holds one end of a long bone firmly in place. The bone begins to crack under the tensile pressure of the sediment pressing downward on the bone.

Figure 2. As the pressure increases, the crack grows larger, angling toward the end of the bone that is fixed in place.

Figure 3. Just before the crack reaches the opposite side of the bone, the force abruptly changes direction. It is still heading downward, but in the opposite direction. Immediately afterward, the bone snaps in two. The change in direction causes the formation of a wedge-shaped breakaway spur. A breakaway spur is always on the surface that was being compressed, and it is always on the segment of bone that was fixed when the crack first opens.

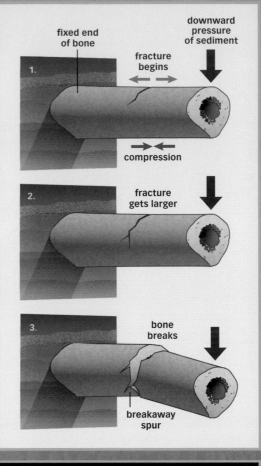

fixed end of bone — downward pressure of sediment

1. fracture begins

compression

2. fracture gets larger

3. bone breaks

breakaway spur

This is Kennewick Man's left tibia. Breakaway spurs on the tibias, a femur, and the left shoulder are consistent with a burial position of Kennewick Man's body lying on his back, with legs stretched straight.

BREAKAWAY SPUR

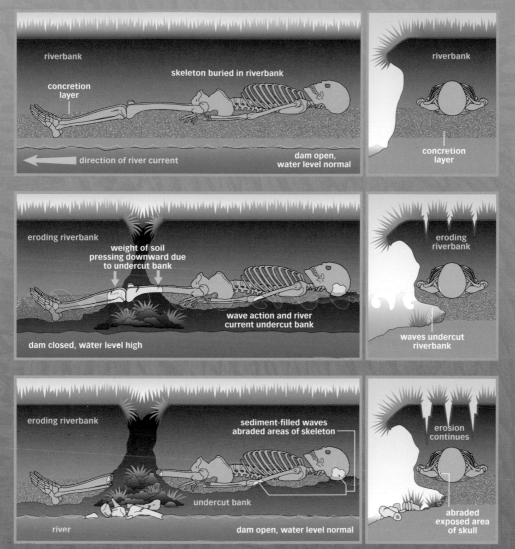

Careful study of different fractures allowed Hugh Berryman to determine the sequence by which Kennewick Man's bones tumbled into the river. The riverbank section that supported Kennewick Man's knees was the first to fall. As the bank eroded, areas of bones became exposed. Sediment-laden water abraded those areas.

Clumps of grass and slumps of sediment litter the shoreline along the base of the bank where Kennewick Man's grave had been.

SOME PERPLEXING GREEN STAINS

While Kennewick Man had answered many questions about his burial and his fall into the river, many still remained. *How long had his remains been in the river? Days? Weeks? Months?* The 1999 study team noticed that green algae stained some of the bones. Algae need two conditions for growth: a wet environment and sunlight. Under favorable conditions, algae may begin growing within one to four weeks. The team concluded the skeleton was on the shore at least several weeks.

The 1999 team also noticed white areas on some of the bones. They attributed this to sunlight bleaching exposed areas of bones while they lay on the shore. A researcher noted that the bleaching occurred over a period of weeks, if not months. The team concluded the bones had been exposed for weeks, if not longer.

When the 2004 study team reexamined the algae, a team member noticed short, green filaments—the threadlike structures of algae—on the surface of two bones. He removed two tiny samples and brought them to James Norris, a biologist who specializes in the study of algae. Norris confirmed the filaments were a kind of algae that grows in freshwater. Equally important, Norris knew how long it takes this kind of algae to colonize, or spread, over an area. In 1996 James Chatters photographed the exposed muddy beach. Algae grew abundantly on the mud, as well as on a large log lying upon it.

If, Norris reasoned, Kennewick Man's bones lay in that area for a long time, a lot of algae would have grown on them too. Then he estimated how long the algae had been growing by measuring the length of the filaments. The limited amount of algae on the bones and the filaments' short length told the 2004 team that Kennewick Man's bones fell rapidly from the bank and lay in the river only one to four weeks.

The 2004 team also reexamined the white areas and reached a different conclusion from the 1999 team. The surface

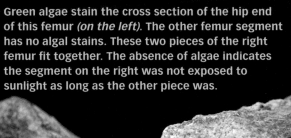

Green algae stain the cross section of the hip end of this femur *(on the left)*. The other femur segment has no algal stains. These two pieces of the right femur fit together. The absence of algae indicates the segment on the right was not exposed to sunlight as long as the other piece was.

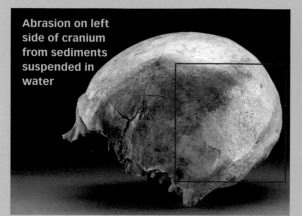

Abrasion on left side of cranium from sediments suspended in water

No abrasion on right side of cranium

color of a bone changes with age, acquiring a darker sheen called a patina. Strong magnification revealed the white patches were places where the patina had been scrubbed off the bone surface. The largest white patches were on Kennewick Man's left side. If he lay on his back with his left side closer to the river—as the 2004 study team believes—these bones would have been among the first exposed. Without the soil's protection, waterborne sediment and debris scoured off the patina, exposing the lighter color beneath.

Each snippet of information brought the 2004 team to new understandings of Kennewick Man and his burial. Had the discovery site not been covered with rocks,

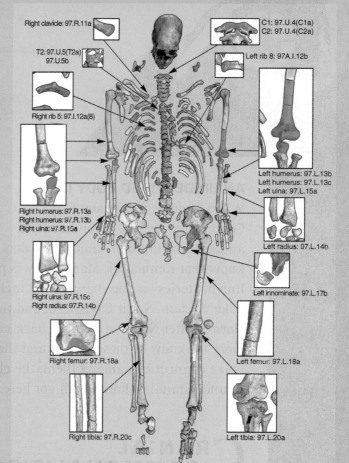

The 2004 team mapped all the algal stains on the bones, helping them determine which bones were exposed longer than others.

Right clavicle: 97.R.11a

C1: 97.U.4(C1a)
C2: 97.U.4(C2a)

T2: 97.U.5(T2a)
97.U.5b

Left rib 8: 97.A.I.12b

Right rib 5: 97.I.12a(8)

Right humerus: 97.R.13a
Right humerus: 97.R.13b
Right ulna: 97.R.15a

Left humerus: 97.L.13b
Left humerus: 97.L.13c
Left ulna: 97.L.15a

Left radius: 97.L.14b

Left innominate: 97.L.17b

Right ulna: 97.R.15c
Right radius: 97.R.14b

Right femur: 97.R.18a

Left femur: 97.L.18a

Right tibia: 97.R.20c

Left tibia: 97.L.20a

the team might have learned more. Not having that context ends part of Kennewick Man's tale, but only part. His story was not finished.

CHAPTER EIGHT

PaleoAmerican Connections

AN UNIDENTIFIED BODY IS AN UNTOLD STORY.
When Thomas and Deacy first found a skull in the
Columbia River, they wondered if that story was
an unsolved murder. Almost two decades later, we
know that Kennewick Man's story is part of a long
line of stories—a line that already includes Arch
Lake Woman, Spirit Cave Man, and the people of
Horn Shelter No. 2—stretching back millennia. The
more we know of these stories and the more we can
make connections among them, the closer we come
to understanding how we all got here.

CRANIAL COMMONALITIES

Looking for connections between Kennewick Man
and other Paleoamericans as well as modern native
peoples was a priority for the 2004 team. Finding
these connections presents a particular challenge,
though. Because each person is different, it's not

possible to define a whole population by a single individual. Instead, researchers must compare individuals to data gathered from known groups and search for similarities.

Anthropologists compare groups of people in two ways. The first is visually. For example, there are forty-eight different skull traits that are visually detectable. They include the shape of the chin, the roof of the mouth, and the nasal aperture (the big opening in the center of the skull between the eyes). A skull with traits in common with hundreds of skulls from a known group is likely to share some ancestry with that group.

The second method reveals differences detected by precise measurement. Thousands of craniums from worldwide groups of people have been measured and entered into a database. The data show that the cranial measurements of people vary, but those measurements of people who belong to a specific population—Chinese or European, for example—vary within a predictable range. And the range of measurements they have differs from those of other populations. The 2004 team measured and visually compared the skulls of Kennewick Man and other Paleoamericans with those from other populations, past and present. How were they different?

The earliest Paleoamericans, including Kennewick Man, Arch Lake Woman, the Horn Shelter people, and Spirit Cave Man, have big skulls in proportion to their overall body size. (It is important to note that cranial shape and size does not reflect the intelligence of a group of people.) From front to back, their craniums are long. From side to side, they are narrow. They have short faces, meaning the distance from the bridge of the nose to the gumline is not very long. Their faces are not as wide as those of Native Americans and recent East Asians, especially across the cheekbones.

In contrast, the size of the skulls of recent Native Americans and recent East Asians is much more in line with the overall proportion of their bodies. From front to back, their craniums are shorter. They are broader side to side. The distance from the bridge of the nose to the gumline is longer than that of the earliest Paleoamericans. And their faces are wider.

Early Paleoamerican populations were diverse, just as modern populations are—for example, there are many different Native American groups. People in one region did not look exactly the same as those many hundreds of miles away. This diversity supports the theory that ongoing migrations occurred, not just one group of founding settlers.

What peoples are the earliest Paleoamericans most like? They share the most similarities with Polynesians and the Ainu. This does not mean they are Polynesian or Ainu. It suggests that the early Paleoamericans, Polynesians, and Ainu have ancient ancestors from the same Asian populations. Spirit Cave Man is most like the Ainu. The 2004 team found Kennewick Man is most like the Moriori, a Polynesian people in the Chatham Islands, near New Zealand, but he is also like the Ainu. Had the ancient ancestors of the Moriori and Ainu lived in coastal areas of mainland Asia fifteen thousand years ago? Did they leave their homeland when people from central Asia migrated to the coast? Because Moriori, Ainu, and early Paleoamerican cranial features differ from recent East Asians (who came from central Asia), it suggests their ancestors did. Over many generations, had they paddled to new homes, some traveling south toward New Zealand, while others coast-hopped in boats northward and finally east to North America? Their skulls and those of the earliest Paleoamericans seem to support this. Proving—or disproving—this theory will be the work of future scientists.

WHERE ARE THEY NOW

So what became of the Paleoamericans? It's likely that some groups of Paleoamericans died out, leaving no descendants. It's also likely that some lived and commingled with different groups—new immigrants—who arrived in later, ongoing migrations from Asia, yet still thousands of years ago. Evidence points to these people as being the direct ancestors of modern Indian tribes. These people were important settlers of the New World, and their descendants are alive today. Exactly how living Native Americans may be related to the earliest Paleoamericans is not yet known. Studying ancient remains could provide the answer.

FACE-TO-FACE

Kennewick Man has shared a lot of information that connects us on a person-to-person level. This connection is further strengthened when science and art join forces and allow us to see him face-to-face.

During the late nineteenth century, scientists examined a number of human cadavers to explore how facial bones were related to the outward appearance of the face. They measured the tissue thickness in key areas—cheeks, chin, and forehead among them—then turned to sculptors for additional help. They used the measurements and considered the scientists' interpretation of facial bones—for example, a prominent chin, heavy browridge, or a broken nose. From this, the sculptors created facial reconstructions for skulls whose identities were either known or suspected. Their results were favorable when compared with portraits and busts of those people. Since then, improved technologies and methods have increased our understanding of facial bone structure and its relationship to appearance, leading to more realistic facial reconstructions. As fans of TV crime shows know, law enforcement agencies sometimes rely on facial reconstructions when seeking public help in the identification of unknown remains. The same process lets today's people "see" our ancient ancestors.

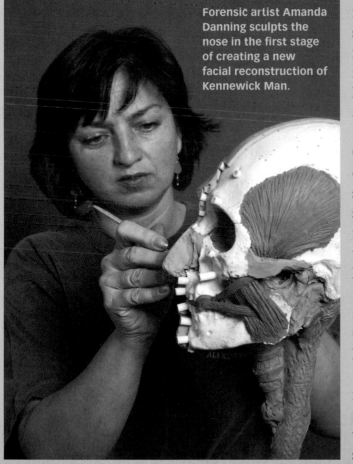

Forensic artist Amanda Danning sculpts the nose in the first stage of creating a new facial reconstruction of Kennewick Man.

In 1996 James Chatters made a replica of Kennewick Man's skull and worked with a sculptor to create a facial reconstruction. Almost ten years later, artist Keith Kasnot created a digital facial reconstruction using a computer program and CT scans of Kennewick Man's skull. In 2010 the 2004 team decided a new reconstruction would be a fitting tribute. "We wanted to use the most recent studies of Kennewick Man's bones and what we've learned from them to show the public what he may have looked like. Because of this, the face differs in some ways from the earlier reconstructions," said Kari Bruwelheide. The team decided a life-size, three-dimensional sculpture of Kennewick Man's head and neck would best depict him.

Since ancient remains are rare, a facial reconstruction is created on top of a precise cast—including all cracks, raised or depressed areas, and natural openings—of the original skull.

The reconstruction was completed in two stages. For the first stage, Owsley and Bruwelheide discussed Kennewick Man's age, physique, possible ancestry, and distinctive skull features with forensic sculptor Amanda Danning. Because no one knows the tissue depth of the skin and facial muscles of Paleoamericans, Polynesians, or the Ainu, Danning created general tissue depths by averaging known tissue depths from southwestern American Indians and Americans of European ancestry who had lived actively, and had been about the same age and weight as Kennewick Man. Input from the anthropologists continued as she shaped the nose, the chin, cheeks, and the forehead. With the cast completely covered and the muscles in place, the reconstruction was ready for stage two: adding details to fully bring the sculpture to life.

StudioEIS is a design and sculpture studio in Brooklyn, New York. StudioEIS sculptors and artists specialize in creating lifelike, naturalistic figures for museums, presidential libraries, and cultural institutions around the world. For more than three decades, StudioEIS has re-created the faces of famous people like George Washington and Abraham Lincoln as well as captured moments in the lives of ordinary people occupied by the tasks of daily life for museums in the United States and abroad.

Owsley and Bruwelheide brought Danning's first-stage reconstruction, plus a second, unaltered, cast of the skull (for skeletal reference), to StudioEIS. They also brought several historic photographs of Ainu and Polynesian men. While it would be inaccurate to say Kennewick Man was an Ainu or Polynesian, many of his features closely resemble theirs. Anthropologists can look at historic images of Ainu and Polynesian men and see how the structure of their skulls is reflected in the forehead, browridges, and the nose. StudioEIS artists saw how the skin of these men became creased on the forehead and around the eyes with age. They individualized Kennewick Man by using these small

Sculpting Kennewick Man at StudioEIS. The skull, photo, and Danning's first-stage reconstruction are close by for reference.

but distinctly important details. The artists knew that Kennewick Man had spent his life outdoors; that he had been exposed to sun, wind, and rain; and that he had suffered from injuries. Based on this information, the StudioEIS' sculptor refined Kennewick Man's cheeks, nose, and brow—even adding a tiny scar above his left eye as a reminder of the healed skull fracture. It's Kennewick Man's gaze, however, that is most startling—it compels eye contact.

The length and style of Kennewick Man's hair are unknown. Ainu photos offered suggestions, but Spirit Cave Man's chin- to shoulder-length hair provided firsthand evidence of an authentic paleohaircut. No one knows if Kennewick Man had a beard and a mustache. Again, based on Ainu photographs, the reconstruction team decided more facial hair, rather than less, was a reasonable assumption.

Painting the sculpture added final realistic touches including hair color and skin tone that reflect not only those of Ainu people but also the weather-beaten appearance of someone who spent a lot of time outdoors. When looking at the new facial reconstruction, one can't help but wonder about Kennewick Man and his life.

THEIR RIGHTFUL PLACE

North America's true human story has greater breadth and depth than we ever imagined. It is far more ancient than Jamestown or Christopher Columbus or even people who lived a thousand years ago. It is a drama far more thrilling than men and women chasing mammoths across frozen plains. Uncovering the whole story, though, takes time and effort, but the valuable tales like those told by Kennewick Man, Arch Lake Woman, the man and girl from Horn Shelter No. 2, and Spirit Cave Man show that it is a worthy pursuit with many unresolved questions for future researchers. These people are rewriting the story of human life in North America. "The essence of a good physical anthropologist is to find what is unique about an individual and then bring it out," says Kari Bruwelheide. Each ancient story she and her colleagues bring out adds a unique thread to the tapestry of North America's story.

Paleoamericans have proven to be astounding educators on topics ranging from science, social studies, math, health, and even art. One critical lesson Kennewick Man continues to teach us is how important it is for scientists and nonscientists to talk with each other. Differences of opinion about Kennewick Man and the conflict between scientists and tribes are an uncomfortable part of his tale. But disagreements can lead to discussions that help us understand other points of view. So disagreement is not necessarily bad. It can be how we learn and grow.

In 1996, after Kennewick Man was discovered, disagreements about the handling of his remains left some Native Americans and some scientists angry. At stake were issues of dignity and respect, as well as honoring ancestors and long-standing tribal traditions. The outcome left some wondering if building a bridge between native peoples and scientists was possible. A recent discovery of human remains at the Upward Sun River site, in central Alaska, is a reason for optimism. Archaeologist Ben Potter meets regularly with local and regional Native Alaskan leaders. So, as soon as he encountered evidence of cremated human remains (baby teeth, specifically slightly shovel-shaped incisors), he contacted tribal leaders. Eager to learn more about someone who may have been an ancestor, the Healy Lake Traditional Council and the Tanana Chiefs Conference sanctioned the excavation and scientific examination of the remains. And the research team and two representatives from the native community held a joint news conference that demonstrated the solidarity of all parties and their common goal of adding to our knowledge about past peoples. This was a long way from the courtroom drama that characterized Kennewick Man's discovery.

As a result of this close collaboration, everyone has been able to meet a Paleoamerican child, who the native community has named Xaasaa Cheege Ts'eniin (haw-SAW CHAG tse-NEEN), which means "Upward Sun River Mouth Child." When the child died, about 11,500 years ago, he or she was only three years old. The child's body was cremated in a cooking hearth located inside a house and not originally intended as a grave. Evidence indicates the body was the last item placed in the fire pit and that the house was abandoned afterward.

This ancient story transports us back in time. We feel a child's death, see a community care for that individual, and empathize with those who lived on despite sadness. Instead of becoming moments forever lost, they add a poignant new chapter to North America's story.

And Xaasaa Cheege Ts'eniin's story may yet continue. DNA samples from contemporary members of the native community have been offered for comparison with that of the child, should DNA prove recoverable. Might this Paleoamerican child have living relatives?

"Scientific research is greatly enhanced by the perspectives of local communities, who bring new questions to the mix, who have real long-term connections to the land, the flora and fauna, and have extensive traditional ecological knowledge of the region. These elements create synergy between researchers and the communities, and ultimately everyone benefits," said Potter. In 2011 two Native Alaskan volunteer archaeologists worked at the Upward Sun River site, and Potter hopes to have many more in the next few years. Maybe a lesson learned from Kennewick Man helped build a bridge at Upward Sun River.

EYES ON THE FUTURE

Kennewick Man and other Paleoamericans teach us that it's smart to have more than one pair of eyes examine a skeleton. When specialists from many scientific fields bring their expertise to a discussion, it stimulates thought and sends us questing for more information. New technologies help us answer old questions and ask new ones undreamed of in the past. One such test, called osteon counting, analyzes structures

If we combine scientific observation, technology, art, and insights from Native American cultures, we—and future generations—can weave a rich tapestry of Paleoamerican life.

in a bone in a way that pinpoints the age of a person at death with increased accuracy. Osteon counting could help determine Kennewick Man's age once and for all. Chemist Marvin Rowe's new technique of radiocarbon dating burns such a miniscule amount of a sample that the area of loss may be detected only with a magnifying lens.

For forty years, people thought the man from Horn Shelter No. 2 was most likely a flintknapper. No one considered the possibility that he might be a healer. No one imagined him playing a drum. Trying to identify a wider range of individual Paleoamerican activities from the stress markers on their bones, markers like the enlarged crests on Horn Shelter No. 2 Man's lower arm bones, is charting new territory.

Thirty-five years ago the peopling of the Americas, according to the Clovis-first theory, was a done deal. Today, we are looking at multiple routes and peoples.

Twenty years ago no one could have foreseen that a collection of bones scattered along a hundred feet (30 m) of muddy shoreline could give scientists enough clues to tell them the deceased person had been intentionally buried by other people. Enough to virtually return that person—Kennewick Man—to his grave. Yet scientists have done just that. But work remains.

The point in Kennewick Man's ilium may be a Haskett point, similar to the one in this photo.

STILL SPEAKING

More than fifteen years after his discovery, Kennewick Man still speaks. In 2012 study team member Dennis Stanford reexamined the stone point in Kennewick Man's ilium. He believes it may be a Haskett point, rather than a Cascade point. The people who made Haskett points were a different culture from those who made Cascade points. They came from areas closer to Idaho. This is a new twist in the story's development. Should the point be a Haskett point, new discussions and questions about exploration and territorial conflicts will arise. Where was Kennewick Man when he received the wound? Who had been the invader, Kennewick Man or his assailant?

More than nine thousand years later, the cause of Kennewick Man's death remains unknown. No bone trauma explains it. Had he sickened from a sudden infection or disease that killed him quickly, before it had a chance to affect his bones? Had he been bitten by a venomous snake? Did he drown? Only future study, plus knowledge and technologies we don't yet have, will answer these questions.

Each Paleoamerican skeleton speaks its own individual story. But if it is combined with those of other people from the same area and time period, they can also speak as a population. This allows scientists to compare groups of Paleoamericans and their descendants. Scientists can see how a population changed in response to environmental stresses. They can observe how genetic traits changed from generation to generation, especially as populations intermingled. Paleoamerican remains are few and far between, reminding us there are many regions and time periods that we know little about, that there is still much to learn. If every ancient skeleton is reburied without being given the opportunity to teach us, we will forever lose the chance to know their people.

We live in a fast-paced world, saturated with round-the-clock video and instant global communication. Still, there's nothing like the power of a great story, even if it takes a long time to unfold. And as storytellers go, Kennewick Man is one of the best. His far-reaching tale provokes thought and imagination. Parts of the tale—hunting with a spear and an atlatl—are unfamiliar to modern humans. Yet others—the pain of an injury—we know well. His right hip is a cautionary tale of at least one conflict between ancient peoples. His skeleton's discovery is a cautionary tale for modern people, one that validates the importance of conviction, yet shows the benefits of compromise.

The amazing thing about Kennewick Man's story is that the more people who participate, the better it gets. When artists, scientists, dentists, teachers, doctors, and even you discover his story and remember him, Kennewick Man's legacy grows. When he dares us to draw conclusions, each of us spins our own line into his story's web. Yet the lines we add must remain flexible to allow room for future revisions, which will further enrich his tale.

Above all, Kennewick Man reminds us that it wasn't stone tools, shell necklaces, atlatls, hearths, or skin boats that began North America's story. It was Paleoamerican *people* who chipped the points, strung the beads, threw the spear, sparked the flames, and paddled the boats. Paleoamericans like Kennewick Man, Arch Lake Woman, the man and girl in Horn Shelter No. 2, Spirit Cave Man, and Upward Sun River Mouth Child. Thousands of years before we took our first breaths, they settled and lived and died here. Paleoamericans were the first human caretakers of the Americas. When their skeletons speak, it is fitting that we, the modern caretakers, should listen. Their stories are the human connection that makes them part of the present and us part of the past. It is the human connection that will carry all of us into the future.

finis

STUDY TEAMS

1999 STUDY TEAM (1998–2001)

JOSEPH POWELL, physical anthropologist

JEROME ROSE, physical anthropologist

GARY HUCKLEBERRY, geologist

JULIE STEIN, geologist

JOHN FAGAN, archaeologist

DOUGLAS DONAHUE, radiocarbon dating

DARDEN HOOD, radiocarbon dating

R. ERVIN TAYLOR, radiocarbon dating

KENNETH AMES, archaeologist; anthropologist

DANIEL BOXBERGER, anthropologist

STEVEN HACKENBERGER, archaeologist; anthropologist

EUGENE HUNN, anthropologist

CLARK LARSEN, physical anthropologist

PHILLIP WALKER, physical anthropologist; bioarchaeologist

DAVID GLENN SMITH, anthropologist; DNA testing

FREDERICA KAESTLE, anthropologist; DNA testing

ANDREW MERRIWETHER, anthropology; DNA testing

FRANCIS P. MCMANAMON, archaeologist

2004 STUDY TEAM (2004–PRESENT)

DOUGLAS W. OWSLEY, physical and forensic anthropologist

HUGH BERRYMAN, forensic anthropologist

DENNIS STANFORD, archaeologist

KARIN BRUWELHEIDE, skeletal biologist; forensic anthropologist

RICHARD L. JANTZ, physical and forensic anthropologist

M. KATHERINE SPRADLEY, physical and forensic anthropologist

CLEONE HAWKINSON, physical anthropologist

D. TROY CASE, physical anthropologist

THOMAS W. STAFFORD, JR., geologist; geoarchaeologist; radiocarbon dating; isotope analysis

GEORGE GILL, physical and forensic anthropologist

C. LORING BRACE, physical anthropologist

MARK TEAFORD, dental anthropologist

BENJAMIN M. AUERBACH, physical anthropologist

CHRISTY G. TURNER II, dental anthropologist

DAVID HUNT, physical and forensic anthropologist

ALEITHEA A. WILLIAMS, Data Management Specialist

DELLA COOK, physical anthropology

DANIEL WESCOTT, physical and forensic anthropology

JAMES NORRIS, biologist

HENRY P. SCHWARCZ, isotope analysis

JAMES CHATTERS, physical anthropologist and archaeologist

REBECCA SNYDER, CT scan–3D modeling

STEVE JABO, molding and casting replica bones

WAYNE SMITH, conservator

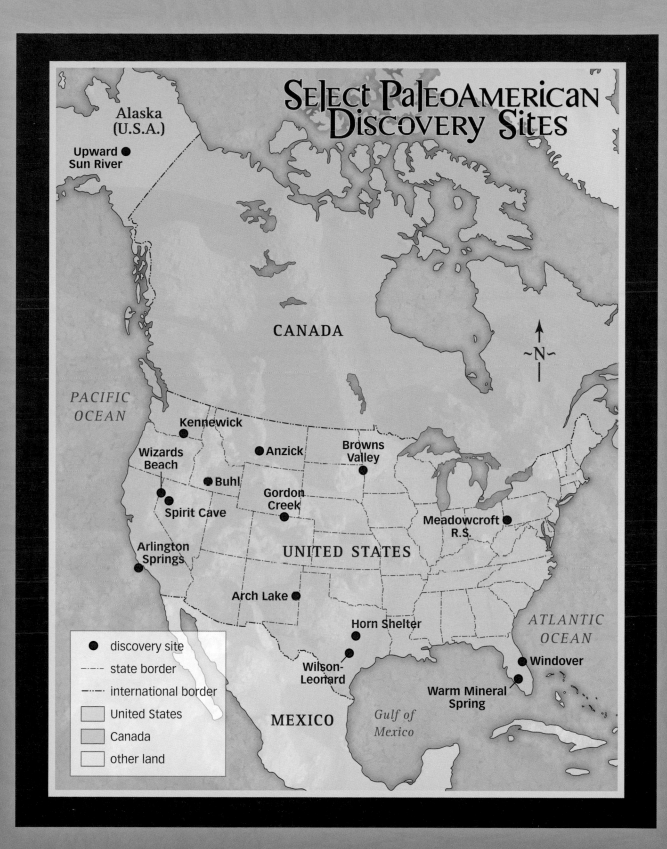

Select PaleoAmerican Discovery Sites

Alaska
(U.S.A.)

Upward ● Sun River

CANADA

~N~

PACIFIC
OCEAN

Kennewick ●

● Anzick

Browns
Valley ●

Wizards
Beach ●
● ● Buhl
Spirit Cave

Gordon
Creek
●

Meadowcroft
R.S. ●

Arlington
Springs ●

UNITED STATES

Arch Lake ●

ATLANTIC
OCEAN

Horn Shelter ●

Windover ●

Wilson-
Leonard ●

Warm Mineral
Spring ●

MEXICO

Gulf of
Mexico

● discovery site
-·-·- state border
-··-··- international border
☐ United States
☐ Canada
☐ other land

129

SOURCE NOTES

8   Will Thomas, interview by Sally Walker, December 17, 2010.

9   Ibid.

12 Ibid.

14 James Chatters, telephone interview by Sally Walker, November 22, 2010.

16 Ibid.

16 Ibid.

16 Ibid.

18 Ibid.

20 Ibid.

21 Ibid.

24 Ibid.

31 Thomas Stafford, e-mail to Sally Walker, December 14, 2011.

31 Ibid.

34 U.S. Department of Justice: Office of Justice Programs, "NamUs National Missing and Unidentified Persons System," n.d., http://www.namus.gov/about.htm (February 24, 2012).

38 John R. Johnson, e-mail to Sally Walker, December 2, 2011.

40 Amy Dansie, e-mail to Sally Walker, January 2, 2012.

44 James Adovasio, e-mail to Sally Walker, December 16, 2010.

44 Dansie, e-mail.

44 *DeKalb (IL) MidWeek,* Looking Back, May 25, 2011.

47   William Billeck, Smithsonian Institution, National Museum of Natural History, Repatriation Office, e-mail to Sally Walker, October 12, 2011.

50 Thomas, interview.

50–21 Claire Chatters, e-mail to Sally Walker, April 18, 2011.

51 Ibid.

52 Native American Graves Protection and Repatriation Act. Public Law 101–601; 25 U.S.C. 3001 et seq.

60 Margaret Jodry, interview by Sally Walker, March 3, 2011.

63 Ibid.

68 Ibid.

66 Margaret Jodry, interview by Sally Walker, March 3, 2011.

66–67 Ibid.

76 Kari Bruwelheide, e-mail to Sally Walker, April 27, 2011.

76 Ibid.

76 Ibid.

77 Ibid.

84 Tom Stafford. Email to Sally Walker, April 16, 2012.

87 Daniel J. Wescott, e-mail to Sally Walker, January 13, 2012.

89 James Chatters, telephone conversation with Sally Walker, December 21, 2011.

101 Wescott, e-mail.

105 Thomas Stafford, e-mail to Sally Walker, April 27, 2011.

106 Ibid.

107 Ibid.

110 Hugh Berryman. Email to Sally Walker, January 1, 2012 119–120   Kari Bruwelheide, interview by Sally Walker, December 12, 2011.

111 Hugh Berryman. Email to Sally Walker, December 30, 2011.

123 Kari Bruwelheide, e-mail to Sally Walker, December 29, 2011.

124 Ben Potter, e-mail to Sally Walker, January 4, 2012.

SELECTED BIBLIOGRAPHY

Adovasio, J. M., and Jake Page. *The First Americans: In Pursuit of Archaeology's Greatest Mystery.* New York: Random House, 2002.

Balter, Michael. "Radiocarbon Datings Final Frontier." *Science* 313, no. 5,793 (September 15, 2006): 1,560–1,563.

Bass, William M. *Human Osteology: A Laboratory and Field Manual of the Human Skeleton.* 4th ed. Special Publications No. 2 of the Missouri Archaeological Society. Columbia: University of Missouri, 1995.

Benedict, Jeff. *No Bone Unturned.* New York: HarperCollins, 2003.

Bonnichsen, Robson, Bradley T. Lepper, Dennis Stanford, and Michael R. Waters, eds. *Paleoamerican Origins: Beyond Clovis.* Center for the Study of the First Americans. Department of Anthropology. College Station: Texas A&M University Press, 2006.

Chatters, James C. *Ancient Encounters: Kennewick Man and the First Americans.* New York: Simon & Schuster, 2001.

——. "The Recovery and First Analysis of an Early Holocene Human Skeleton from Kennewick, Washington." *American Antiquity* 65, no. 2 (April 2000): 291–316.

Dixon, E. James. *Bones, Boats, & Bison: Archeology and the First Colonization of Western North America.* Albuquerque: University of New Mexico Press, 1999.

——. "Coastal Navigators." *Discovering Archaeology* (discontinued publication of *Scientific American*), January–February 2000, 34–35.

Faure, Gunter. *Principles of Isotope Geology.* 2nd ed. New York: John Wilcy & Sons, 1986.

Fried, Stephen. "Who Were the First Americans?" *Chicago Tribune*, June 13, 2010.

Gill, George W., and Rick L. Weathermon, eds. *Skeletal Biology and Bioarchaeology of the Northwestern Plains.* Salt Lake City: University of Utah Press, 2008.

Gruhn, Ruth, ed. *Who Were the First Americans?* Proceedings of the 58th Annual Biology Colloquium, Oregon State University, Robson Bonnischsen, ed. Center for the Study of the First Americans. Ellsworth, ME: Downeast Graphics & Printing, 1999.

Habu, Junko. *Ancient Jomon of Japan.* Cambridge: Cambridge University Press, 2004.

Jodry, Margaret A. "Walking in Beauty: 11,000-Year-Old Beads and Ornaments from North America." *Bead Forum* 57, no. 1 (2010): 6–9.

Libby, Willard F. "History of Radiocarbon Dating," In Conference Proceedings: Symposium on Radioactive Dating and Methods of Low-level Counting, Monaco (Monaco), 2–10, March 2–10, 1967. Vienna: International Atomic Energy Agency. Available online at http.//www.osti.gov/accomplishments /documents/fullText/ACC0336.pdf (January 10, 2011).

Lowery, Darrin L. *Geoarchaeological Investigations at Selected Coastal Archaeological Sites on the Delmarva Peninsula: The Long Term Interrelationship between Climate, Geology, and Culture.* PhD dissertation, University of Delaware, 2009.

Meltzer, David J. *First Peoples in a New World: Colonizing Ice Age America.* Berkeley: University of California Press, 2009.

Owsley, Douglas W. and Richard Jantz, eds. *Kennewick Man: The Scientific Investigation of an Ancient American Skeleton.* College Station: Texas A&M University Press, forthcoming.

Owsley, Douglas W., Margaret A. Jodry, Thomas W. Stafford Jr., C. Vance Haynes Jr., and Dennis J. Stanford. *Arch Lake Woman: Physical Anthropology and Geoarchaeology.* College Station: Texas A&M University Press, 2010.

Owsley, Douglas W., and Richard L. Jantz. "Archaeological Politics and Public Interest in Paleoamerican Studies: Lessons from Gordon Creek Woman and Kennewick Man." *American Antiquity* 66, no. 4 (October 2001): 565–575.

Potter, Ben, Joel D. Irish, Joshua D. Reuther, Carol Gelvin-Reymiller, and Vance T. Holliday. "A Terminal Pleistocene Child Cremation and Residential Structure from Eastern Berengia." *Science* 331, no. 6,020 (February 25, 2011): 1,058–1,061.

Powell, Joseph F., and Jerome C. Rose. "1999 Report on the Osteological Assessment of the 'Kennewick Man'

Skeleton (CENWW.97.Kennewick)." *National Park Service.* http://www.nps.gov/archeology/kennewick/powell_rose.htm (October 19, 2010).

Redder, Albert J., and John W. Fox. "Excavation and Positioning of the Horn Shelter's Burial and Grave Goods." *Central Texas Archeologist* 11 (1988): 2–15.

Reimer, Paula, Mike G. L. Baillie, Edouard Bard, Alex Bayliss, J. Warren Beck, Paul G. Blackwell, C. Bronk Ramsey, et al. "2009 IntCal09 and Marine09 Radiocarbon Age Calibration Curves, 0–50,000 Years Cal BP." *Radiocarbon* 51, no. 4 (2009): 1,111–1,150.

Rowley, William D., ed. *Nevada Historical Society Quarterly* 40, no. 1. (Spring 1997), 1–140.

Stanford, Dennis J. and Bruce A. Bradley. *Across Atlantic Ice: The Origin of American's Clovis Culture.* Berkeley: University of California Press, 2012.

Thomas, David Hurst. *Skull Wars: Kennewick Man, Archaeology, and the Battle for Native American Identity.* New York: Basic Books, 2000.

Trope, Jack F., and Walter R. Echo-Hawk. "The Native American Graves Protection and Repatriation Act: Background and Legislative History." *Arizona State Law Journal* 24, no. 1 (Spring 1992): 35–77.

Tykot, R. H. "Stable Isotopes and Diet: You Are What You Eat." In *Proceedings of the International School of Physics* "Enrico Fermi" Course CLIV. Edited by M. Martini, M. Milazzo, and M. Piacentini. Amsterdam: IOS Press, 2004, 433–444.

Walker, Phillip L., Clark Spencer Larsen, and Joseph F. Powell. "2000 Final Report of the Physical Examination and Taphonomic Assessment of the Kennewick Human Remains (CENWW.97.Kennewick). September 6, 2007. *National Park Service.* http:www.nps.gov/archeology/Kennewick/walker.htm (October 19, 2010).

Waters, Michael R., and Thomas J. Stafford Jr. "Redefining the Age of Clovis: Implications for the Peopling of the Americas." *Science* 315, no. 5,815 (February 2007): 1,122–1,126.

FURTHER READING

Allaroundnevada.com
http://wwwallaroundnevada.com/?p=190
This site is a panorama of Spirit Cave that virtually takes the viewer on a tour inside the cave.

CalPal: Cologne Radiocarbon Calibration & Palaeoclimate Research Package
http://www.calpal-online.de/
To calibrate radiocarbon years into calendar years, visit this website.

Center for the Study of the First Americans
http://www.centerfirstamericans.com/index.php
Department of Anthropology at Texas A&M University hosts this website. It includes information about past and ongoing Paleoamerican research projects. It is a good source for additional websites offering additional information about paleoamerica.

Halls, Kelly Milner. Mysteries of the Mummy Kids. Minneapolis: Millbrook Press, 2007.

A Journey to a New Land
http://www.sfu.museum/journey
This site features interactive videos concerning Paleoamerica presented at various educational levels.

Murray, Elizabeth A. Forensic Identification: Putting a Name and a Face on Death. Minneapolis: Twenty-First Century Books, 2012.

National Park Service
http://www.nps.gov/nagpra
This website contains information about NAGPRA and the various legislations and hearings about its establishment.

Texas Beyond History
http://www.texasbeyondhistory.net/
This website offers detailed information about Horn Shelter No. 2 and other prehistoric discoveries in Texas.

INDEX

AUTHOR ACKNOWLEDGMENTS

GETTING TO KNOW KENNEWICK MAN HAS BEEN A RARE PRIVILEGE.
The ongoing research needed to write this book was more than trips to the state of Washington or to Washington, D.C. It involved examining the skeleton, photographing its features, and then reexamining the photographs countless times. Each time Doug held one of the bones was like transcending time, a true window opened to the past. In the past months, we discussed Kennewick Man's life, often acting out activity-related gestures to better understand their effect on his muscles and bones. Mentally, we put ourselves in his shoes. Telling the story made us think outside the box, using art and even music, in addition to standard scientific approaches. Critically analyzing the data took—in fact is still taking—many thousands of hours of work. In a very real sense, Kennewick Man has become part of our lives, and we thank him for doing so. We also thank Arch Lake Woman, Spirit Cave Man, and the Man and Girl from Horn Shelter No. 2 for all they've taught us. There would be no story without them.

We could not have told their ancient stories without the help of many modern people. They deserve profuse thanks. Will Thomas, Dr. James Chatters, and Claire Chatters shared a wealth of information about the early days of Kennewick Man's discovery. Dr. Thomas Stafford supplied assistance over and above the call of duty on radiocarbon dating, isotopes, and geological interpretation. Dr. Marvin Rowe added breaking news about minimally destructive radiocarbon dating techniques. Dr. James Adovasio and Amy Dansie provided information about paleotextiles and Spirit Cave. Dr. Richard Jantz worked with Doug in skeletal assessment. Dr. Mark Teaford sunk his teeth into helping us understand paleoteeth. Dr. John Johnson clarified Arlington Springs Man. Dr. Daniel Wescott explained bone response to activity. Darrin Lowery brought the story of the Cinmar blade to our attention. Margaret Jodry and Dr. Dennis Stanford offered new slants on old occupational thoughts, and Dr. Erin Walker Bliss gave Sally a lesson in hand drumming. Dr. Hugh Berryman deftly explained the mechanics of bone fracture. Laurie Burgess and William Billeck, at the Smithsonian, and David Selden, at the National Indian Law Library, supplied information about repatriation and NAGPRA. Dr. Ben Potter shared material about the Upward Sun River site. Kari Bruwelheide identified and assessed skeletal features, but she added more than scientific information to our tale; she also added heart.

For pulling information and photos together, a virtual bouquet goes to Vicki Simon, Cass Taylor, and Aleithea Williams. A bow to Andrew Karre, patient editor and software sensei, and a gold pencil to Laura Westlund for creating concrete illustrations of images that previously existed only in our minds. A thankful nod to agent Ken Wright.

Last, but not least, we thank our families, particularly our spouses, Susie and Jim. We can't begin to count the times they've heard "be there in just a minute"—which often turned into hours—when we were occupied with Kennewick Man-related tasks.

ABOUT THE AUTHORS

SALLY M. WALKER is the author of many award-winning books for young readers. Her *Secrets of a Civil War Submarine: Solving the Mysteries of the* H. L. Hunley won the American Library Association's prestigious Sibert medal in 2006. She is also the author of *Written in Bone: Buried Lives of Jamestown and Colonial Maryland, Frozen Secrets: Antarctica Revealed,* and *Blizzard of Glass: The Halifax Explosion of 1917.* When she isn't busy writing or doing research for books, Ms. Walker works as a children's literature consultant. She lives in DeKalb, Illinois.

DOUGLAS W. OWSLEY is a curator and the division head of physical anthropology at the Smithsonian's National Museum of Natural History. He is one of the foremost forensic anthropologists in the world. His work has ranged from identifying the victims of serial killers to reconstructing some of the oldest skeletal remains in North America. He has published many books, but *Their Skeletons Speak* is his first work for young readers. He lives in Culpeper County, Virginia.

PHOTO ACKNOWLEDGMENTS

The images in this book are used with the permission of: National Museum of Natural History, Smithsonian Institution (NMNH)/courtesy of Doug Owsley, photos by Chip Clark: p. 2, 15, 17, 19 (all), 21, 45, 48 (both), 55, 61 (bottom), 74 (both), 77 (both), 78, 79, 80, 81, 83, 85, 90, 92, 94 (both), 95, 97 (both), 99 (both), 102 (both), 107, 109 (both), 111, 112 (bottom), 114, 115 (top left, top right); photos taken at the Nevada State Museum, pp. 32, 33 (bottom), 41(all), 43; photos taken at the Blackwater Draw Museum, Eastern New Mexico University, pp. 58, 61 (top), 108 (top); special thanks to Albert Redder and the Texas Archeological Research Laboratory, pp. 64, 65 (both), 66 (both), 67, 69, 84 (right), 108 (bottom); photos taken at the National Museum of Health and Medicine, p. 96 (all). NMNH/courtesy of Doug Owsley, photos by Brittney Tatchell, pp. 13 (right), 122 (sculpture by StudioEIS); NMNH/courtesy of Doug Owsley, photo by Donald E. Hurlbert, p. 119. Additional images: © David Frazier/CORBIS, p. 7; © James Chatters, pp. 9, 71, 113 (bottom); © Laura Westlund/Independent Picture Service, pp. 10, 12, 14, 30, 35, 63, 112 (top), 113 (top), 129; © Nigel Corrie/ English Heritage Photographic Studio, p. 13 (left); © Peter Endig/dpa/CORBIS, p. 23; Thomas Burke Memorial Washington State Museum, # 45N14/305 #1983-14, p. 24; © Howard Goldbaum, http://www.allaroundnevada. com, p. 26 (both); Images by Sydney and Georgia Wheeler, Nevada State Museum, Carson City, pp. 28, 29, 33 (top left, top right); NMNH/courtesy of Dennis Stanford, photo by Chip Clark, p. 36; Santa Barbara Museum of Natural History, Bones in situ 1960, photographed by Phil Orr, p. 37; © Sally Walker, p. 39 (top); Courtesy of Darrin Lowery, p. 39 (bottom); NMNH, p. 47 (left, center); National Anthropological Archives, Smithsonian Institution, BAE GN 00125/Bell Collection 06640300, p. 47 (right); © Claire Chatters-Elf, p. 51; El Llano Archaeological Society, James Warnica, Cecil Clark, Greg Moore and F.E. Green, pp. 56, 57; Courtesy of Albert Redder and the Texas Archeological Research Laboratory, University of Texas at Austin, p. 68; © Ira Block/National Geographic/Getty Images, p. 84 (left); Courtesy of Dr. Daniel Wescott, pp. 87, 88 (both); © Joseph H. Bailey/National Geographic/Getty Images, p. 100; Courtesy Thomas Stafford, Stafford Research Laboratories, Colorado, p. 106; NMNH/illustration by Alice Tangerini, p. 115 (bottom); George Montandon, Au Pays des Ainou. L'Anthropologie, 1927, p. 121 (inset); Photos by StudioEIS, pp. 121 (main), 125; © Idaho Museum of Natural History, p. 126. Cover images: NMNH/courtesy of Doug Owsley, photos by Chip Clark.